GW00702340

BRITISH RAILWAYS' STEAM LOCOMOTIVES

F. G. Cockman

Shire Publications Ltd

Published in 1998 by Shire Publications Ltd, Cromwell House, Church Street, Princes Risborough, Buckinghamshire HP27 9AA, UK.
Copyright © 1980, 1990 and 1998 by F. G. Cockman. First published 1980. Second edition 1990. Third edition 1998. Number 5 in the History in Camera series. ISBN 0 7478 0372 2.
F. G. Cockman is hereby identified as the author of this work in accordance with Section 77 of the Copyright, Designs and Patents Act, 1988.
All rights reserved. No part of this publication may be reproduced or transmitted in any form or by any means, electronic or mechanical, including photocopy, recording, or any information storage and retrieval system, without permission in writing from the publishers.

British Library Cataloguing in Publication Data: Cockman. F. G. (Frederick George), 1902-. British Railways' steam locomotives. – (History in camera; 5). 1. Steam locomotives – Great Britain – History – 20th century. I. Title. 625.2'61'0941'09045. ISBN 0 7478 0372 2.

Cover: *Western Region 4-6-0 number 6004 'King George III' at Iver on the up 'Red Dragon' on 2nd December 1961. (Photograph: 'Colour Rail')*

Previous page: *The modern version of the mixed traffic locomotive arrived with C. B. Collett's Hall class 4-6-0 'Saint Martin', number 4900, in 1924. The type proved such a useful 'maid of all work' that 329 were turned out from Swindon, including the later Modified Halls. Number 5923 'Colston Hall' is pictured on the Bournemouth to York express on 11th April 1961. This was the 14.40 from Oxford, on a very cold spring day, so that the exhaust could barely lift itself over the roof of Wolvercot signalbox. No engine looked smarter than a clean Hall with its coat of Brunswick green and polished metalwork.*

Contents

Preface 4
Introduction 5
Express locomotives 7
Mixed traffic locomotives 25
Tank locomotives 41
Freight locomotives 62
Places to visit 77
Index 79

On the Great Northern Railway H. A. Ivatt introduced his small Atlantics in 1898 and the larger type in 1902. The latter, although sluggish in their original form, were transformed by Gresley from 1913. Ninety-four of the larger type were built, the last surviving until 1950. One of each type has been preserved. Number 3301 (later 2829) is shown on an up express near Sandy in 1937, in the standard apple-green finish.

Preface

Steam reigned so long as the prime mover on the railways of Great Britain that, up to 1939, it seemed it would go on for ever. It is true there was a cloud, no bigger than a man's hand, which first appeared in 1934, when the Great Western Railway introduced its diesel railcars, and in 1936, when the 0-4-0 diesel shunters began to work on the London Midland & Scottish Railway. On 1st January 1948 the British Transport Commission took over more than two hundred different types of steam locomotive, and between 1951 and 1960 it produced twelve additional types. Yet by 1968 all had gone. There is no need to go into the various reasons here as they are due more to politics than to engineering. Fortunately steam enthusiasts can console themselves by visiting the National Railway Museum in York and many other museums up and down Britain. Furthermore they can still see and hear the locomotives working and, better yet, travel behind them on the many preserved railways. In this book over one hundred steam locomotive types are depicted and described, and these belong to the more important and interesting designs as obviously there is not room for them all.

I acknowledge the kindness of the Oxford Railway Publishing Company Ltd for permission to quote from *Mendip Engineman* by P. W. Smith and also from *Firing Days* and *Footplate Days* by Harold Gasson. Also I am indebted to Ian Allan Ltd for their agreement to my quoting from *Locomotive Panorama* by E. S. Cox and from *Locomotive Adventure* by H. Holcroft.

The photographs are my own, with a number of exceptions, which are acknowledged as follows: K. C. H. Fairey, pages 9 (top), 22, 23 (bottom), 26 (top), 35, 49 (bottom), 54 (bottom), 61 (bottom), 63 (top), 67 (bottom), 70, 71 (bottom); L. A. Hanson, pages 3, 9 (bottom), 14 (bottom), 26 (bottom), 43 (bottom), 62; G. A. Richardson, page 52 (bottom), 74 (bottom); the late J. B. Sherlock, pages 11 (bottom), 19 (bottom), 32, 37 (top), 52 (top).

Bedford   F. G. COCKMAN

Introduction

One of the most interesting facts which emerge from the study of the steam locomotive is that the Stephensons were basically correct in their design of the *Rocket*. The principles which guided George and Robert Stephenson – a multi-tubular boiler, cylinders mounted on the frame and forced blast – showed a complete departure from the colliery locomotives hitherto in use. When they improved the breed by integrating the firebox with the boiler, mounting the cylinders horizontally and using expansion valve gear, they set a pattern which endured for 115 years. There were of course many other locomotive engineers such as Hackworth, Woods, Gooch and Kirtley, and the last mentioned became famous in 1858 when he invented the brick arch in the firebox to enable the Midland Railway engines of the time to consume the smoke produced when burning coal. Since that time there have been progressive steps like compounding, higher boiler pressures made possible by better metal, piston valves and superheating. Improvements were also made in the locomotive as a vehicle with the use of bogies and pony trucks. When the British principle of railway travel had been established abroad, it became the turn of foreigners to make their contribution. Such items as the Belpaire firebox, Walschaerts valve gear and the Schmidt superheater come to mind, and later on the de Glehn bogie and valve gears by Lentz and Caprotti. At the end of the steam era attention was directed to improving the draughting by such famous inventors as Le Maitre, Kylala, Chapelon and Giesl. But all the time the Stephenson basis was there, and, as E. S. Cox has stated in his interesting *Locomotive Panorama,* such diversions as multi-cylinder sleeve valve engines and steam turbines showed no improvement in coal consumption and reliability.

   The fact that railways were built under private enterprise in Great Britain led to the formation of hundreds of companies, both great and small, many of them having their own individual locomotive types. In spite of amalgamations there were still 123 separate companies in 1922, and these had to be reduced to four groups by the Railways Act (1921). This fusion dated from 1st January 1923, and the groups inherited a diversity of locomotives developed over the years by locomotive engineers who were largely uncommunicative with each other. Even after 1923 the four groups went their own ways as regards design, but nevertheless steam reached its high peak in the years leading up to 1939. The Transport Act 1947 put an end to private ownership, but notwithstanding this the four groups continued to manufacture their own engines, and even in 1956 the Western Region produced nine

GWR pannier 0-6-0Ts. As from 1951 R. A. Riddles had put on the road
the new British Standard steam locomotives, each being a synthesis of
the best of the former group designs, and these continued to appear
until 1960, when the last three 2-10-0s left the works. The last was
number 92220 *Evening Star* from Swindon. During this period the
army of steam engines was still enormous as the British Transport
Commission inherited over 3500 from the Great Western, 7300 from
the London Midland & Scottish, 6200 from the London & North Eastern and 1850 from the Southern. To this collection Riddles added 999
of his own design.

This book sets out to describe and illustrate some of the most interesting or the most important types of steam locomotive to be seen at
work during the final reign of steam, the period 1948 to 1968. It is
convenient to divide steam engines into four main classes – main line
express, mixed traffic, tank and freight. It is simple but rather arbitrary
as an express locomotive can haul freight trains, mixed traffic engines
are designed to tackle almost anything, tank engines can often take
over heavy work but are limited by their fuel capacity, and freight
locomotives can at times work passenger trains quite satisfactorily

Express locomotives

In the early days of railways the term 'express engine' was not used because there was only one type and the managements were satisfied if the trains could depart and arrive on time. After all, the railways had no need to hurry as their superiority over the horse-drawn coach was demonstrated by the slowest trains. For example, the *Times* coach from Bedford used to leave for London, in 1845, at 8.30 and arrive about five hours later. The single fare was £1. By 1846 the public could leave by the LNWR station and after changing at Bletchley arrive at Euston in two and a half hours, the cost being 25p. Another reason for low speed was the Edward Bury 0-4-0 type, very undersized, with which the London & Birmingham and the Midland Counties railways were afflicted in 1838 and 1839. It was competition between the railways themselves that forced an increase in speed, and the express type of locomotive was developed. In 1845 the Gauge Commission was sitting to decide whether the standard gauge of 4 feet $8^{1}/2$ inches (1436 mm) or the broad gauge of 7 feet $0^{1}/4$ inch (2140 mm) should prevail, and to demonstrate their superiority the Great Western management sent their 2-2-2 locomotive *Ixion* with a light train from Paddington to Didcot in 63 minutes. This average of 50 miles per hour (80 km/h) necessitated a maximum of 60 mph (96 km/h). Nevertheless, the standard-gauge supporters won the day by virtue of the extent of their railways already laid, showing a superiority in mileage of ten to one.

Furthermore, the time soon arrived when a monopoly of service was broken. The London & Birmingham's route to Birmingham was the only one from 1838 until 1852, when the Great Western arrived. Similarly the Great Northern was able to run trains to York (via Askern Junction) in 1850, thus breaking the hold of the Euston Confederacy on that town, and by 1860 the London & South Western Railway was able to convey passengers to Exeter, over which route the Great Western had enjoyed sole rights since 1844. All this rivalry led to the development of the express passenger locomotive, which made possible the 'race' to Edinburgh in 1888, and a similar contest to Aberdeen in 1895.

By the end of the nineteenth century, then, most railways were depending on the 4-4-0 type for their expresses, the designs being strong and reliable rather than spectacular. Drummond's T9 4-4-0 for the London & South Western in 1899 was notable for its solid build and its speed, and the class was worth rebuilding by Urie in 1922. In 1900 James Holden had produced the celebrated *Claud Hamilton,* number 1900, and subsequent members of the class managed trains weighing 400 tons daily, although this required careful maintenance, the best coal and picked crews. The Midland Compound, dating from 1902 and later

T9 4-4-0 number 30120 at Halwill Junction on 8th May 1961, shortly to depart with the 14.43 stopping train to Exeter. The fireman can be seen on the tender filling up with water. These were Drummond's most successful express engines, earning the name of 'Greyhounds', and sixty-six were built from 1899. The original green livery gave place to lined black in BR days.

modified, was another successful design, showing up well in the 1923 trials on the LMSR by its low coal consumption. In 1919 Maunsell had rebuilt the handsome Wainwright E1 4-4-0s and in 1921 he turned his

S. W. Johnson brought out his most powerful express engine for the Midland in 1902. It was a 4-4-0 compound on the Smith system. At first five were built, and they showed so much promise that Johnson's successor, Deeley, built another forty with modifications. Finally the LMS added 195, making a total of 240. They lasted until 1961, when number 41198 was withdrawn. Here, number 41143 is seen at Bedford (Midland Road) on a stopping train to St Pancras in September 1957. This is a lined black livery, adopted in 1948.

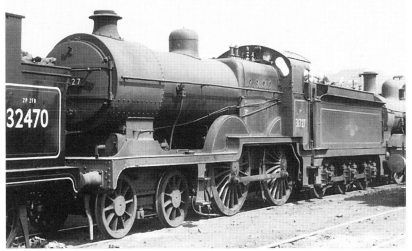

Class D1 4-4-0 locomotive number 31727. In 1901 H. Wainwight, Chief Mechanical Engineer of the South Eastern & Chatham Railway, designed one of the handsomest express locomotives ever seen in Britain. However, by 1921 the class could no longer cope with the heaviest duties and was rebuilt by R. E. L. Maunsell with superheaters, long-travel piston valves and Belpaire boilers. The result was a much more powerful engine with little extra weight. They were at work until 1961. This one was photographed at Ashford on 4th June 1959.

attention to the D1 class. In each case a great increase in power was achieved with an increase in weight of only 1 ton.

At the turn of the century the Great Western led all the others in terms

The Midland Railway used small engines to haul short but frequent trains. Hence the large number of Class 2 4-4-0s. Many were Johnson designs rebuilt by Fowler, and others were built by him from 1928. BR inherited 242 of the class. Number 40500 is seen at Burton on Trent on 9th May 1948. They lasted until 1963.

of speed and design efficiency. G. J. Churchward was already applying his principles of high pressure, long lap valves with long travel and generous steam passages. His City class had appeared in 1903, and the next year *City of Truro* achieved 100 mph (160 km/h) and more when descending Wellington Bank. The last of all the 4-4-0s was Maunsell's Schools class, the first of which was built in 1930. These modern three-cylinder locomotives performed wonderful work on the difficult Hastings and Portsmouth routes, and fortunately two have been preserved.

It was a logical step to increase the power of a 4-4-0 by turning it into a 4-6-0, and the 4-6-0 subsequently became the backbone of train operation in Great Britain, with the exception of the LNER. On the Highland Railway in 1894 Jones had produced his 4-6-0 'Goods', which was really a most capable mixed traffic engine. But the transition was not a simple one, and several famous locomotive superintendents fell down in the process. Drummond's T14 4-6-0 was never as good as his T9 4-4-0; McIntosh's celebrated *Cardean* was only fractionally better than his superb Dunalastair IV class. On the Great Central James Robinson produced a magnificent 4-4-0, the Director, but his 4-6-0 types were disappointing. Other designs which could have been better were Hughes's on the Lancashire & Yorkshire and Bowen-Cooke's on the LNWR,

Schools class number 30939 'Leatherhead' prepares to leave Tonbridge with the 14.10 train to Hastings on 2nd September 1960. The Schools were one of Maunsell's great successes and did great work on Portsmouth and Hastings express trains. Forty were built from 1930, and twenty-one were fitted with the ugly but efficient Le Maitre chimney. Their rank entitled them to lined green livery.

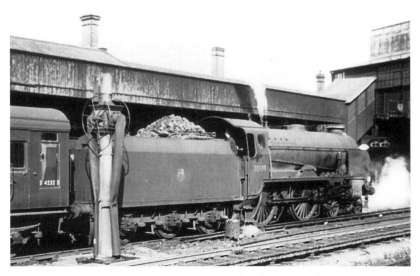

In 1923 C. B. Collett produced the Castle class 4-6-0, held by many to be the handsomest and most efficient express engine to run in Britain. Here we see number 5025 'Chirk Castle' at Oxford on 23rd July 1962 returning to shed. The livery was the normal Brunswick green lined out. The tender is the largest type with 4000 gallons of water and 7 tons of coal. No fewer than 167 Castles were built up to 1950.

The Kings appeared on the GWR four years after the Castles. Thirty were constructed to work the Birmingham and Plymouth expresses and had the normal GWR livery of green with copper-topped chimney and brass beading to the splashers. The picture is dated 1939 and shows number 6004 'King George III' on a West of England express. The attractive single chimney was replaced by a double chimney in the 1950s as a result of tests made at Swindon by S. O. Ell.

R. E. L. Maunsell scored a great triumph with his King Arthur class of 4-6-0. The first appeared in 1926 and was a modification of the Urie N15 class with thoroughly modern steam distribution. Seventy-four were constructed. The illustration shows number 30795 'Sir Dinadan' at Brighton in the usual Southern finish of malachite green, on 27th August 1959. It had just worked an excursion train from Brent via Kew and Factory Junction.

although in this case Bowen-Cooke was compelled by the Civil Engineer to adopt a smaller boiler than he wished. The Claughton was a near miss on the target of success. On the Great Eastern the 1500 class of 4-6-0, brought out during the regime of S. D. Holden, repeated the success of the 'Clauds'. Between 1905 and 1930 the Great Western was in the ascendant, and this railway continued to bring out superb 4-6-0s, under both Churchward and Collett.

In retrospect it seems strange that Churchward was the only Chief Mechanical Engineer before the First World War who really appreciated the essential features for his designs – high boiler pressure, long travel valves and an unobstructed steam circuit. Built with these points incorporated, the Star 4-6-0 of 1907 was an immediate success, which was repeated in 1923 with Collett's Castle and again with his King in 1927. It is a rare instance of a locomotive going straight into production off the drawing board. In the meantime at Ashford, Maunsell, who had recruited some of his staff from Swindon, took the Urie N15 and gave it higher pressure, smaller cylinders and long travel valves. The result was the celebrated King Arthur 4-6-0, which performed so well on the Dover and Plymouth trains until the coming of Bulleid in 1937. The first, number E453 and named *King Arthur,* underwent its trials in 1925, but in 1926 another 4-6-0 was constructed, this time using four cylinders.

Maunsell's most imposing design was the 'Lord Nelson' type 4-6-0. Number 859 'Lord Hood' was built in 1929 and for a time had smaller driving wheels, 6 feet 3 inches (1905 mm) instead of 6 feet 7 inches (2007 mm). Bulleid improved their performance by fitting new cylinders and the Le Maitre multiple-jet blast pipe.

One of the interesting things about locomotive design is that there is no guaranteed road to success. The new engine, E850 *Lord Nelson,* was a delight to the eye, but its performance was disappointing. Harry Holcroft in his excellent book *Locomotive Adventure* hints that details of the design were worked out at Eastleigh, far away from Maunsell. E. Roger Arnold, who was in the erecting shop at Eastleigh in 1926, told the author that there was difficulty in assembling the valve gear and on the last night Maunsell himself visited the shop at 2 a.m. to see if all was going well. The story is an unfortunate one because Maunsell, in order to make thorough tests, built only one example and after a year reported to the board of directors that he was satisfied. Their reply was that extensive electrification was in hand, and authority was given to build only fifteen more. Engine crews thought that the eight soft exhausts per revolution of the driving wheels did not 'lift' the fire off the bars sufficiently, and one was converted to the normal four beats. Other modifications were made, and in 1938 Bulleid made a great improvement in their performance by fitting new cylinders and a multiple jet exhaust.

To the north of the Thames the railways were having to face the same needs for more power arising from heavier and more comfortable rolling stock and for more speed to beat road competition. On the London & North Eastern Railway the 4-6-0 type had never been adopted for the most important trains, although Gresley put in hand, in 1928, the three-cylinder B17 class, the first batch being built by the North British Locomotive Company. They did well on the Great Eastern main line from Liverpool Street, and later on the former Great Central from Marylebone. To save weight, the frames were reduced in thickness and this told against the engines after twenty years' good service. The London Midland & Scottish Railway had to face the same problem, and in 1927 they also turned to the North British Locomotive Company for seventy Royal Scots. They were able to haul the heaviest expresses until the Pacifics arrived in 1933. In 1943 the Royal Scots were converted under Stanier and became rivals to the Castles in efficiency, if not in looks. Three years after the Scots, the LMS turned out the Patriot class, three-cylinder like the Scots, but slightly less powerful. Their reputation is best summed up by that great LMS driver Laurie Earl, who remarked to the author: 'The Patriots are as fast as the Scots and more economical in fuel. They are my favourite engine.' In 1934 Stanier decided to produce his own version of the Patriots by bringing out the Jubilees. But success eluded this handsome design despite several modifications, and the answer was not found until after 1942. However, they were a good second-line engine.

The building of express engines was discouraged during the Second World War although mixed traffic types were permitted. In 1945 F. W. Hawksworth produced the excellent County 4-6-0 with driving wheels

In 1928 Gresley brought out a new 4-6-0 design to improve the haulage power on the former Great Eastern and Great Central railways. The picture shows number 2814 (61614) 'Castle Hedingham' on an express to Clacton on 6th August 1933. They looked most attractive in their apple-green finish and bore the names of East Anglian towns and mansions and later of football teams.

Class 6 4-6-0 number 45543 'Home Guard' at Camden shed on 14th August 1954. Fifty-two engines were turned out to the designs of Sir Henry Fowler and were known as the 'Patriot' class, dating from 1930. The livery was Brunswick green lined out. The last went in 1962.

Carlisle Upperby shed used to house a large number of the Royal Scot class 4-6-0, and this is a view of number 46116 'Irish Guardsman'. The engines appeared during the Fowler regime in 1927 but were rebuilt from 1943, the first rebuild being number 46103 'Royal Scots Fusilier'. The photograph was taken on 5th May 1957 and shows the engine with double chimney and livery of lined Brunswick green, dating from August 1944.

6 feet 3 inches (1905 mm) in diameter, which entitled it to be termed mixed traffic. It did well in Cornwall and between Wolverhampton and Chester, provided it was intelligently driven like a two-cylinder engine. The pressure was 280 pounds per square inch and it was to be the basis of Hawksworth's Pacific. Unfortunately the nationalisation of the railways prevented the building of the Pacific.

The next logical step would have been the 4-8-0 type, as André Chapelon was to demonstrate later on the SNCF. But already, in 1908, the Great Western Railway had turned out the first Pacific to run in Great Britain. With four cylinders *The Great Bear* was really a lengthened Star, and it can be argued that it was not necessary. But anyone who saw it in full flight on a Bristol express would agree that it constituted a splendid advertisement for the GWR. It could also be argued that the streamlined casing on the Gresley A4 was unnecessary, but it was good advertising and attracted thousands of passengers to the LNER. That is what railway management is all about. In 1924 *The Great Bear* was converted into a Castle as the original boiler needed heavy repair, but two years earlier an imposing Pacific had appeared from Doncaster in the form of Gresley's number 1470 *Great Northern*. It had little difficulty in carrying out its appointed task, the haulage of 600-ton trains at 60 mph (96 km/h), but the coal consumption was heavy, and it appeared that the 1925 locomotive exchange was necessary to bring

Jubilee class 4-6-0 number 45599 'Bechuanaland' at Carlisle Upperby on 5th May 1957. This was Stanier's 1934 design for secondary expresses and no fewer than 191 were constructed. In 1942 number 5736 'Phoenix' was fitted with modified exhaust and double chimney to improve steaming; later number 5735 'Comet' was given similar treatment. The pre-war LMS lake gave place to BR Brunswick green.

F. W. Hawksworth became Chief Mechanical Engineer of the GWR in 1941, and in 1945 he produced the County class of 4-6-0. Thirty duly appeared in the GWR Brunswick green. Here number 1028 'County of Warwick' is seen at Bristol Temple Meads on 20th June 1957 awaiting its next turn of duty. They had the latest design of tender – 4000 gallons of water and 7 tons of coal.

home the need for up-to-date cylinder and valve design. Also in 1922 the Raven 4-6-2 was turned out at Darlington. When Gresley was convinced that the A1 class needed modification he set about it, and the A3 was the result. This impressive engine set the fashion for high-speed running with economy that was to be characteristic of LNER performance.

The authorities at Crewe were aware of what was happening, and Stanier built the *Princess Royal,* a four-cylinder Pacific, surely one of the finest-looking locomotives to take the rails. This was in 1933, but number 6200 and the sister engine 6201 *Princess Elizabeth* required some alterations before they developed their best style. The royal occasions in 1935 (Silver Jubilee of King George V) and 1937 (coronation of King George VI) encouraged the chief mechanical engineers to make further efforts. Gresley's answer was the amazing A4 and the 'Silver Jubilee' train, and two years later Stanier had his streamlined Princess Coronation Pacifics on the West Coast main line. The year 1937 saw the 'Coronation' express on the East Coast main line, and the 'Coronation Scot' on the West. They were immensely popular. The 'Coronation' had a beaver-tail observation coach at the rear, and after the 16.00

One of the most famous of preserved locomotives is number 4472 'Flying Scotsman'. It belonged to the LNER A3 class, in which Gresley had combined efficiency and good looks. It bore the number 60103 for a time. The photograph depicts the engine drawing an enthusiasts' special at Sharnbrook on 11th September 1965.

Doncaster multiplied the number of the A3 class until seventy-eight were in service. As on other regions, the quest for efficiency led to modifications of the locomotives that were not always pleasing to the eye. Number 60056 'Centenary', seen on 25th July 1962, is about to go to Top Shed. They were finished in BR Brunswick green and lined out.

The celebrated A4s appeared in 1935 to run the streamlined Silver Jubilee train, and they were so successful that thirty-five were built. One, number 4469 'Sir Ralph Wedgwood', was destroyed at York by enemy action but the remaining thirty-four lasted to the end of steam. They were Gresley's chef d'oeuvre. Number 60017 'Silver Fox', one of the first four silver engines, is waiting at Hitchin on 3rd July 1962 with the 17.15 stopping train from King's Cross.

After his appointment to Crewe in 1932 Stanier set about designing a powerful express engine to take over the heaviest work from the Royal Scots. The twelve Princess Royals had beautiful lines, and the LMS lake livery looked just right. After boiler alterations they were able to deal with the most exacting duties. Here is number 46205 'Princess Victoria' at Camden 'Loco' in 1959. This one had a rocking grate, and they all looked well in the later Brunswick green.

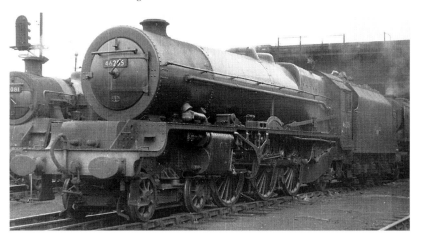

A development of the Princess Royals (46200 and 46201, 46203 to 46212) was known as the Princess Coronation, later the Duchess class. According to the fashion of the time, forty-three out of fifty-five were streamlined, but the casings were removed by 1946. At this time three more Pacifics were built, numbers 46202, 46256 and 46257. The liveries were as for the Princess Royals. The photograph depicts number 46223 'Princess Alice' at Crewe on 9th August 1951.

A great deal of attention was aroused by the first of the Merchant Navy class in 1941 owing to the unusual appearance. Thirty were built, but under BR all were rebuilt, commencing with number 35018 'British India Line' in 1956. Number 35003 'Royal Mail' is seen leaving Basingstoke on 15th October 1964 at the head of the Pines Express, which had been diverted from the S&DJR from 10th September 1962. Whether in Southern or BR green, they are a memorial to the genius of O. V. Bulleid.

In 1945 there appeared the West Country or Battle of Britain class, a smaller version of the Merchant Navy class. Out of the 110 examples BR rebuilt sixty, commencing with number 34005 'Barnstaple' in June 1957. Number 34050 'Royal Observer Corps' (rebuilt) is at Waterloo on 29th April 1965, ready to take the 13.54 stopping train to Basingstoke. The livery is BR green.

Peppercorn A1 Pacific number 60156 'Great Central' running into Grantham on 29th August 1961 with the 14.49 express to King's Cross. The design originated in 1946, and five locomotives, including number 60156, were fitted with roller bearings. The others were 60153, 60154, 60155 and 60157. As turned out in Brunswick green fully lined out, the family of fifty looked most impressive.

A2 class 4-6-2 locomotive number 60529 'Pearl Diver' at New England on 26th May 1957. This class, numbering forty in all, was A. H. Peppercorn's adaption of Thompson's A2/1 design. With 6 foot 2 inch (188 cm) driving wheels, it was a very useful mixed traffic design, being both speedy and powerful. The last example was withdrawn in 1966, but fortunately number 60532 'Blue Peter' has been preserved.

departure from King's Cross passengers hurried over their tea and congregated in the beaver tail. From this vantage point one could see the signals snap back to danger just as the tail passed them, and stations, bridges and tunnels disappeared into the distance at a most impressive rate.

There were no more Pacific designs until Bulleid's of 1941, when the Merchant Navy appeared in its air-smoothed casing, and 1945, which saw the similar West Country.

The high noon for steam travel was the decade 1930-9, when A4 *Mallard,* number 4468, achieved its 126 mph (203 km/h), thus beating 6220 *Coronation,* which had touched 114 mph (183 km/h). There was a revival after 1954 on the Western Region when 7018 *Drysllwyn Castle* and 6015 *King Richard III* comfortably exceeded 100 mph (160 km/h). This speed was also achieved by 35012 *United States Line* on the Southern Region. One defect of the Pacific type was its tendency to slip on starting, particularly on a wet day. The Great Western 4-6-0 was very sure on its feet at all times.

The Transport Act of 1947 had set up the British Transport Commission to take over all forms of inland communications in the form of road, canal and rail traffic, with a Railway Executive to manage the last mentioned. With R. A. Riddles at the head, two Pacific designs were put forward, and in 1951, three years after the formation of the Executive, the Britannia class 4-6-2 commenced duties. The first engine, number 70000, was named *Britannia*, and several were sent to the

Three years after nationalisation in 1948 R. A. Riddles produced the first BR Pacific, number 70000 'Britannia', and in all fifty-five were built. They performed sterling work on the Liverpool Street to Norwich trains and on the Victoria to Dover boat trains. Here number 70024 'Vulcan' is pictured on humble freight work near Wolverton on 17th October 1962. They were most impressive in their BR uniform of lined green, although not every shed kept them clean.

BR Standard Class 6 4-6-2 number 72006 'Clan Mackenzie' at Stranraer in 1962. Only ten were built in 1952 as the wider use of the 'Britannias' and the excellence of the Class 5 4-6-0s made the class unnecessary. The last was withdrawn in 1966.

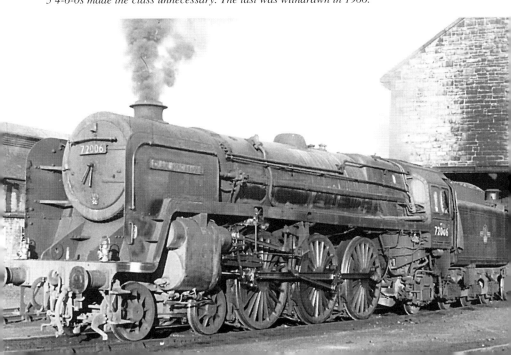

Great Eastern line, where they showed themselves easily capable of working the Liverpool Street-Norwich two-hour expresses. Number 70004 did equally good work on the 'Golden Arrow' Victoria-Dover train, and they were found all over Britain. They had a mixed reception on the Western Region, but in conversation with the author one Old Oak Common driver said: 'The Britannias can run away from a Castle and are lighter on coal and water.' In 1952 a smaller Pacific was built and ten of them were named after Clans. They worked mostly in Scotland and the North of England.

The last 4-6-2 design was number 71000 *Duke of Gloucester*, which emerged from Crewe works in 1954. This three-cylinder Pacific was much more powerful than the Britannia and performed well, although burning coal rather excessively. Any proposed research was, however, abandoned when the 1955 Modernisation Plan indicated that the future lay with diesel power. The arguments against steam power – smoke pollution, unattractive daily servicing and the expense of coal – were cogent, but the real reason surely is that modern speeds require 4000 horsepower to maintain them, and the best Pacific could not offer more than 2500.

Mixed traffic locomotives

During the nineteenth century the express passenger locomotive and the freight locomotive had developed along the conventional lines into well-defined groups, but at the same time it was felt that there should be types which could do either work. Thus Patrick Stirling and William Adams designed 0-4-2 tender engines that proved most useful for the Great Northern and London & South Western Railways respectively. On the Great Eastern James Holden brought out the celebrated T26 2-4-0 in 1891, of which ninety were built. But they were not large engines, and although the obvious step would have been to design the 2-6-0 class it is usually accepted that the unspectacular 2-6-0 engines imported from the Baldwin and Schenectady works in the USA in 1899 made British engineers less than enthusiastic. These ran on the Midland, Great Central and Great Northern railways.

In 1912 Gresley turned out his first creation, an 0-6-0 with 5 foot 8 inch (1727 mm) driving wheels; although capable of mixed traffic work, these engines were rather rough at high speeds. Just before this, Harry Holcroft of Swindon had been to Canada and had seen the extensive use

The first true mixed traffic engine appeared in 1911 on the Great Western when G. J. Churchward authorised the design. So successful was number 4301 that the class multiplied to a total of 322, and 217 were inherited by BR. Number 6395, dating from 1924, was based on Aberystwyth shed. They were painted in Brunswick green and were coupled to the type of tender with a capacity for 3500 gallons of water and 6 tons of coal.

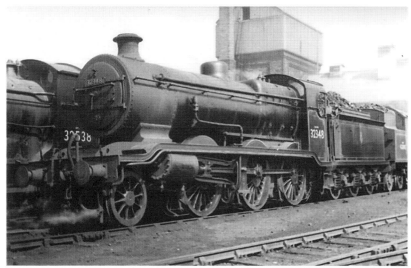

The 2-6-0 wheel arrangement became popular in 1911 when it was introduced by the Great Western. The Great Northern followed in 1912, and in 1913 L. B. Billinton produced a design for the London Brighton & South Coast Railway. The illustration shows number 32348 at Three Bridges on 17th April 1955. It was a member of a group of seventeen, which lasted until 1962.

made of the 2-6-0 type. His favourable report reached Churchward, who said: 'Very well then, get me out a 2-6-0 with 5 foot 8 inch wheels, bringing in all the standard details you can.' This is recorded in Holcroft's *Outline of Great Western Locomotive Practice.* So, in 1911, was born the first of the true mixed traffic types. Other lines followed suit, thus

The example of the GWR in constructing the 2-6-0 type for mixed traffic locomotives was followed by the Great Northern in 1912 when Gresley's Mogul appeared. This was later known as K2, and number 4681 (later 61771) is shown at Sandy on a freight train on 1st May 1937. Seventy-five examples were produced, all having black livery.

In his K3 2-6-0 locomotive (1920-4) Gresley planned much better steam distribution, and this three-cylinder machine was capable of drawing heavy freight and fast passenger trains. They were used a great deal on the former Great Central line, and the illustration is of number 61824 leaving Finmere on 22nd March 1961 with the 13.09 stopping train to Marylebone. The total number turned out was 193, and they looked well in black paint lined out.

The need for a powerful mixed traffic engine had been felt on the South Eastern & Chatham Railway as far back as 1917, and the Chief Mechanical Engineer, R. E. L. Maunsell, brought out the N class with the help of assistants drawn from Swindon. Number 31831 was waiting in a siding at Penshurst on 2nd September 1960. At first in green livery, they finished their days in the usual lined black. Eighty were built.

The London Midland & Scottish Railway used the 2-6-0 type extensively, and the 1926 version is attributed to both Hughes and Fowler. Number 42872 is depicted at Millbrook at the head of a freight train on 29th July 1961. The finish was in black, and 245 were built, including five with poppet valves.

the Gresley K2 2-6-0 of 1912 for the Great Northern and L. B. Billinton's handsome K class of 1913 for the London Brighton & South Coast. R. E. L. Maunsell for the SECR devised the N class in 1917, to be followed by a three-cylinder version, the N1, in 1922, thus beginning his work of thorough modernisation.

In the meantime a most imposing engine had emerged from Doncaster. Gresley's new K3 three-cylinder 2-6-0 caused universal comment with its 6 foot (1829 mm) diameter boiler. The designer must have taken note of the valve travel on the GWR 4300 class, as his 1920 K3 was very modern in this respect. Number 1000 and its followers at once took over a variety of duties, and during the coal strike of 1921 they dealt successfully with heavy expresses. However, at speeds in the range of 80 mph (129 km/h) the valves would be reciprocating six times a second, and this velocity, combined with whip in the derived gear, caused the centre valve to overrun. Gresley cured this in his first Pacific by shortening the valve travel, and this spoiled a fine engine. More of the K3 class appeared in 1924.

A very efficient 2-6-0 had been planned by G. Hughes for the LMSR, but they were built under the rule of Sir Henry Fowler. They first took the road in 1926 and were soon called 'Crabs' as their high inclined cylinders presented an unusual appearance. The large 21 inch (533 mm) cylinders had to be raised to conform with the loading gauge. They performed yeoman service until the end of steam.

When planning his N class 2-6-0 in 1917, Maunsell also decided on a tank-engine version, and Ashford produced a good-looking and powerful 2-6-4T, number 790. Twenty were made and named after rivers. Unfortunately, number 800 'River Cray' was derailed at Sevenoaks in 1927, and Maunsell decided to rebuild them as tender engines. Thus arose the excellent U class 2-6-0 in 1928, and thirty were added to the twenty tank engines so rebuilt. Number 31802 is shown at Yeovil Pen Mill on 10th October 1962. They wore lined black livery.

The Southern Railway system presented a suitable case for fast trains to be hauled by powerful tank engines, and a three-cylinder version of the K class 2-6-4T number 790 was developed by Maunsell in 1926. This was numbered A890, and the valves for the inside cylinder were operated by a combination of the two outside sets of Walschaerts gear. This engine was also rebuilt as a 2-6-0 in 1928, class U1, and twenty more such locomotives were built later. The view of number 31896 on a coal train is at Three Bridges on 23rd March 1961. The finish was in lined black.

In 1917 Maunsell had designed at Ashford a handsome and efficient 2-6-4T locomotive designated class K. Twenty were built in all and given the names of rivers. They did excellent work, but in 1927 one of them was derailed at Sevenoaks. As for the cause, Harry Holcroft suggested that the Southern Railway's shingle ballast shifted under the weight, while E. Stewart Cox thought that the movement of the pony truck and the bogie should have been more restricted. These points are reviewed in their books *Locomotive Adventure* and *Locomotive Panorama* respectively. Another feature was the surging of water in the tanks owing to lack of baffles. Unfortunately there was the usual trial by the daily press, and the board of the Southern decided to have the engines rebuilt with tenders. Thus the U class came into being, and fresh examples were built, all giving good returns to the Southern Railway and the Southern Region. A three-cylinder tank engine, number 890, class K1, was also rebuilt and gave rise to the class U1, equally excellent.

The Stanier version of the 2-6-0 or Mogul was inaugurated in 1935, but it was less distinguished than that produced by his successor in 1945. H. G. Ivatt was responsible for a 2-6-0 mixed traffic locomotive that was good enough to form the basis of the later BR Standard version.

Another LMS 2-6-0 design began in 1947 when H. G. Ivatt produced his own version. The first few had ineffective double chimneys, but these were removed and a very useful engine resulted. They went all over the country, and number 43095 was at Horncastle on 18th September 1962. There were 162 of these lined black locomotives.

The Railway Executive, set up by the Transport Act 1947, drew up a schedule of locomotive types to be built to the designs of R. A. Riddles. Several mixed traffic types were placed in service, including the class 2 2-6-0, which was numbered in the 78000 series. This is number 78002, built in 1953, and depicted shunting at Barmouth on 3rd September 1957. They were very little different from Ivatt's LMS 2-6-0 engines, and all sixty-five were finished in lined black.

Another Riddles design was the class 4 2-6-0, numbered in the 76000s. This was also begun in 1953, and many found their way to the former Great Central Railway. Number 76042 is at Neasden depot on 14th October 1961 after finishing its day's work. 115 engines were turned out in the usual livery

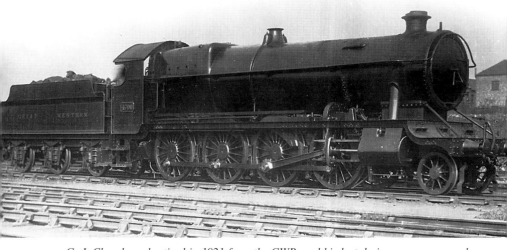

G. J. Churchward retired in 1921 from the GWR, and his last design was an unusual 2-8-0 mixed traffic engine. They were numbered 4700-8 and were excellent either on freight or on semi-fast passenger trains. Had Churchward been younger, no doubt he would have multiplied this class, but his successor, C. B. Collett, preferred the 4-6-0 as a mixed traffic locomotive. These engines were finished in GWR green, and the picture shows the first of the class at Acton in 1929, in its tenth year of service.

This was in 1947, and in the same year a smaller class 2 engine emerged. This was also most successful. It could be said that the 2-6-0 classes 4 and 2, numbered 76000 and 78000 onwards, brought out by Riddles for the nationalised railways in 1953, were direct derivatives of Ivatt's engines.

Despite its omnipresence the 2-6-0 engine had its limitations. Some chief mechanical engineers saw the need for a locomotive with a longer chassis to take an enlarged boiler and to accommodate a bogie at the leading end as being better adapted to high speed. Hence the impressive Churchward 2-8-0 dating from 1919 with 5 foot 8 inch (1727 mm) driving wheels. They were most useful, but only nine were built at the end of Churchward's career, and his successor, C. B. Collett, preferred the 4-6-0. In 1936 Gresley amazed the engineering world by creating the 2-6-2 type with number 4771 *Green Arrow*. Its first duty was the 15.40 fast goods from King's Cross, and the numbers increased each year. They were remarkable engines, able to take over expresses from the Pacifics as required and to haul heavy freight. The only drawback was their weight, and with a route availability of 9 their scope was limited. To have a more available type, Edward Thompson designed a K1 2-6-0 in 1945, and its route availability was rated at 6. With two cylinders, this locomotive was better suited to post-war conditions. After 1945, maintenance was not of a high standard and two-cylinder engines were preferred to those with three. Some idea of conditions applying to locomotive depots after 1945 may be deduced from remarks made by a shedmaster during a conversation: 'I have a staff of

The problem facing the railways during the Second World War and thereafter was maintenance, and Edward Thompson rightly chose to employ two cylinders on his locomotives, except in the most powerful types – hence his excellent K1 2-6-0 dating from 1945. Seventy-one were constructed by him and his successor, A. H. Peppercorn. Number 62002 was photographed at Doncaster in 1959. They were attractive in lined black and could work over most of the LNER system.

Gresley's policy of designing powerful locomotives placed the LNER in a strong position before 1939, and during the war the haulage power was vital. His V2 2-6-2 of 1936 was as powerful as a Pacific and almost as fast. 184 were put to work, but their weight limited them to certain parts of the line (route availability 9). They were favoured with green livery, and number 60826 is shown passing Sandy on 3rd March 1961.

R. W. Urie designed his S15 4-6-0 mixed traffic locomotive in 1920, and in 1927 Maunsell brought out his own version with improved valve events. Others were built in 1936, but this handsome and useful class never exceeded forty-five in number, partly because of extended electrification. Number 30840 is shown standing at Clapham Junction on 15th April 1960, and this example has a short chimney and eight-wheeled tender. Livery is black.

LNER B16 4-6-0 number 61453 on a freight train at York on 10th May 1960. Some designers felt that mixed traffic work required a locomotive more capable of high speed and more stable than a 2-6-0. Sir Vincent Raven used a three-cylinder 4-6-0 (NER class S3), which became LNER class B16, the first representative appearing in 1920. Sixty-nine examples were constructed, and Gresley improved seven of these by rebuilding. Enginemen, however, preferred the subsequent Thompson rebuild with three sets of Walschaerts gear. The B16s had the usual mixed traffic uniform of black, lined out.

forty-seven men, only three of whom are English.' It is not difficult to appreciate that, in these conditions, the proper servicing of the Gresley derived gear was almost impossible.

The best form of mixed traffic locomotive was the 4-6-0, and early forms were represented by the Immingham class on the Great Central and the S1 and S2 on the North Eastern, both in the first decade of the twentieth century. After the end of the First World War Urie set himself the task of providing the London & South Western Railway with a stock of simple up-to-date locomotives, and for mixed traffic he designed the S15 4-6-0. This was in typical Urie robust form with traditional valve motion, but few were built as he retired in 1922. The first appeared in 1920, and in the same year Sir Vincent Raven produced his excellent S3 (LNER B16). But for the modern version of the mixed traffic 4-6-0 we must again turn to Swindon. In 1924 C. B. Collett decided to replace the 6 foot 8$^{1}/_{2}$ inch (2045 mm) driving wheels of the Saint class number 2925 *Saint Martin* with ones of 6 feet (1829 mm) only. This rebuild was the first of the famous Halls, of which large numbers were turned out, and a modified type was constructed under Hawksworth. It was undoubtedly the success of the Hall that prompted Stanier to produce his Black 5, and their manufacture ran into hundreds. Sir William Stanier will always be remembered by his great successes – the Duchesses, the Black 5s and the 2-8-0 8Fs. Between the Hall and

LNER B12 4-6-0. This type was introduced on the Great Eastern Railway as S69 in December 1911. It was rebuilt under the Gresley/Thompson regime in 1932, with round-topped boiler and long travel valves. Eighty were built, the last going in 1961. The photograph depicts number 61545 at Norwich in 1956. Number 61572 has been preserved.

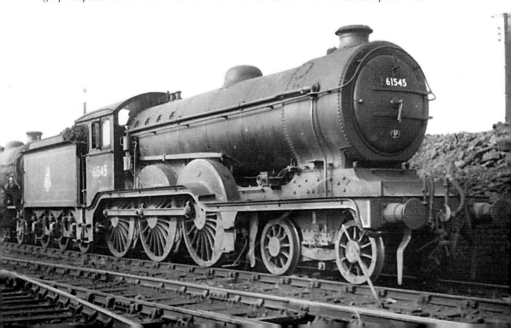

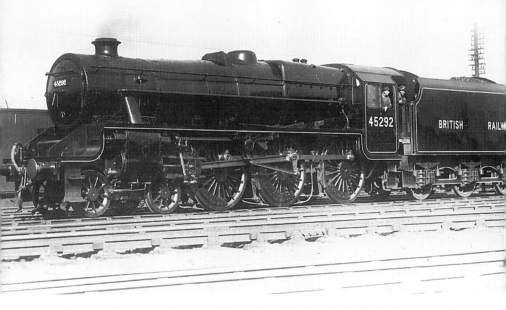

Some new locomotives have required considerable alterations before being accepted for traffic, and others have been right from the start. Amongst the latter are the famous Stanier class 5 4-6-0 (Black 5), and they were so useful that 842 were turned out, between 1934 and 1951. The photograph shows number 45292 at Willesden in 1949. The finish was lined black.

The driver's view from the footplate of class 5 4-6-0 number 45379, on 11th March 1965. It is at the head of the 14.10 train from Aylesbury to Nottingham Victoria, and the starting signal has just been cleared.

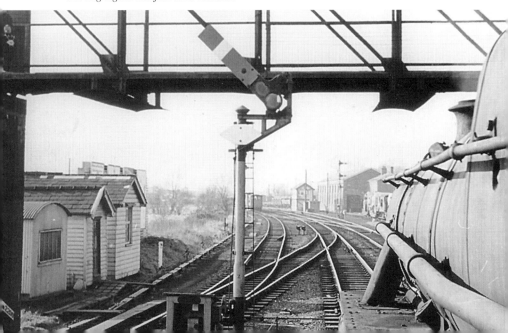

The Granges followed the Halls in 1936 and, with a driving wheel diameter 4 inches (100 mm) less, proved to be a speedy and economical class. Number 6805 'Broughton Grange' is shown near Theale in 1937 on freight work. This family numbered eighty in all, with finish similar to that of the Halls.

The Manors appeared in 1938 and did good work in Wales. Number 7827 'Lydham Manor' waits at Welshpool with the down Cambrian Coast Express on 29th April 1958. The class totalled thirty in the usual green.

In 1942 Edward Thompson supplied the LNER with a much needed mixed traffic engine having a wide range of action. The route availability was RA5. The total built was 410. Number 61357 is seen at the head of the Miners' Gala special train passing St Margaret's, Edinburgh, on 7th July 1963. The final withdrawal of the B1 class was in 1968.

the Black 5 Maunsell had as usual put the seal of perfection on the S15 by his 1927 example. During the Second World War certain types took the brunt of the enormous number of special trains, notably the Halls on the Great Western, the class 5 on the London Midland & Scottish and Gresley's V2 on the London & North Eastern. Valiant work was done on the Southern too, but with a greater variety of classes – the N and N1, the U and U1 and the S15s. They were described by the crews according to the region as 'the engines which won the war', and this had the ring of truth about it. In 1936 Collett decided that there was a case for a 4-6-0 with even smaller wheels, and the Grange class appeared in that year. They were also numerous, and it is always worthwhile hearing what the enginemen thought of the different types. In his *Footplate Days,* Harold Gasson, who was at Didcot shed, says: 'The Grange could be relied upon to do the same work as the Hall but with much less coal.' Two years after the Grange yet another 4-6-0 emerged from Swindon. This was the smaller Manor class, with all the good looks of the Halls and the Granges. Although mixed traffic in size, its usual work was on passenger trains along the route of the former Cambrian Railways. There are many fine photographs of a Manor on the 'Cambrian Coast Express' in Wales. They used to run as far as Shrewsbury.

The appearance of Thompson's B1 4-6-0 on the LNER in 1942 was noteworthy because this type was rare on that railway. The palmy days of before 1939 had gone from the railways for ever, and the LNER, never a rich line, was faced with unsatisfactory conditions for the main-

The extensive range of mixed traffic locomotives designed by R. A. Riddles for BR included a class 4 4-6-0. The first appeared in 1951, and in 1957 a variation was tried with double blastpipe and chimney. All those working on the Southern Region were so treated. Here is number 75069 at East Grinstead on 23rd March 1961 with the 15.40 to Victoria. Eighty were built with the normal livery.

The BR range naturally included a class 5 engine, and the first of the family, number 73000, is here seen being serviced at Bedford 'Loco' on 8th March 1957. Building went on from 1951 to 1957, and the final number was 172, all in lined black. Attention should be drawn to the excellent design of tender fitted to the BR Standard engines, giving a good view when running tender first, with a minimum of coal dust.

tenance of the Gresley type of three-cylinder engine and with the need for an engine with a low route availability rating. It must have occurred to the Chief Mechanical Engineer, Edward Thompson, that the company would benefit from a standardisation scheme for locomotives such as was operating successfully on the LMSR and the GWR – hence the B1 4-6-0, which had a route availability rating of 5, and which was built in hundreds by Peppercorn after Thompson's retirement. The B1 did very well in the 1948 trials, and they all lasted, with the exception of number 1057, until the end of steam. In fact, in 1968 a B1 was still being used to supply steam as a stationary boiler. At first they appeared gradually and were used on secondary duties, and *Blackbuck* (later 61006), shedded at Peterborough, certainly lived up to its name as it scampered across the fens to March. Their acceleration was noticeably better than that of the venerable Claud Hamiltons which they displaced.

The list of 4-6-0 locomotives is brought to a close by mention of the two BR Standard types which took up their duties in 1951. The class 5 engines, numbered from 73000, were not an exact copy of the Stanier Black 5 as they had another $1/2$ inch (13 mm) on the cylinder diameter and 2 inches (51 mm) on the diameter of the driving wheels. They proved to be a powerful and speedy design and worked all over Britain. They showed the modern trend for a strong uncomplicated locomotive having two outside cylinders with valve motion operated direct from Walschaerts gear. A few were fitted with poppet valves, which most enginemen found gave very free running but lacked the essentially fine variations in cut-off. A new departure was the class 4 engine, which proved to be extremely useful. It could show a good turn of speed on the Euston and St Pancras suburban trains, 80 mph (129 km/h) being easily within its powers. On the Southern Region the locomotives were fitted with double chimneys, apparently with some benefit.

This, then, is a summary of the principal mixed traffic engines to be found between 1948 and 1968. They were truly 'maids of all work' and were the backbone of railway operation.

Tank locomotives

The railways of Great Britain were always great users of tank engines, and travellers abroad noticed that, for example, in Spain, shunting was carried out by ancient but well preserved tender locomotives, often of British origin. In a densely populated country like the United Kingdom, with towns near each other, the tank engine was ideal, and it had no need of turntables. Most of our examples were long-lived, and some of Stroudley's Terriers are at work after a life of over one hundred years. They date from 1872, and the first to be built worked on the East London Railway and later on the South London Railway. They were named after places on the Brighton line. Although the pretty outside cylinder 4-4-0Ts of the North London Railway, built by Adams in 1868, have all gone, there remains one specimen of J. C. Park's 0-6-0T dating from 1879. Continuing the 0-6-0T story, this time on the Great Eastern Railway, there appeared in 1890 a type which was equally at home on the dense suburban traffic to Enfield or Chingford and on goods traffic. They were created by J. Holden, and one, number 87, is at the National Railway Museum. H. A. Ivatt's 0-6-0ST of 1897 and W. Worsdell's side-tank version of 1898 were required to perform shunting and freight duties, whereas S. W. Johnson's model of 1899, continued by Deeley and Fowler with better cabs, were used both on passenger

The longevity of the steam engine is emphasised by this picture of number 30586 shunting at Wadebridge on 5th May 1958. This type was the creation of W. G. Beattie in 1874, and three survived into BR days. They were painted plain black.

W. Stroudley's Terrier 0-6-0Ts became famous in their day and operated on the South London line and also where weight restrictions applied, such as on the Hayling Island branch. The first appeared in 1872, and fifty were built at Brighton. Several have been preserved, notably number 55 'Stepney', here waiting at Sheffield Park station on 25th March 1963. At first painted in umber, and later in lined black, 'Stepney' has had the original coat restored by the Bluebell Railway.

J. C. Park was Locomotive Superintendent of the North London Railway in 1879, and it was he who designed this powerful outside cylinder 0-6-0T. Thirty were built at Bow and were always painted black. The one survivor is depicted at Sheffield Park on the Bluebell Railway. It was numbered 76 and also 116 by the NLR, 2650 by the LNWR, 7505 and 27505 by the LMSR, and finally 58850 by BR. It is preserved as number 2650 and was photographed on 27th July 1962.

At Wolverton there were four ancient carriage shunters bearing a plate 'Carr. Dep. Wol', dating from 1870. Originally designed by Ramsbottom, they were rebuilt by F. W. Webb. The photograph is of one of these engines of the 0-6-0ST type working on 19th June 1957. They were all black.

S. W. Johnson introduced a useful 0-6-0T type in 1899, one of which, number 7238, is shown at Derby. The class proved so efficient that Sir Henry Fowler added 417 to the original sixty. After 1948 the engine was renumbered 47238. The class lasted to almost the last days of steam in 1967.

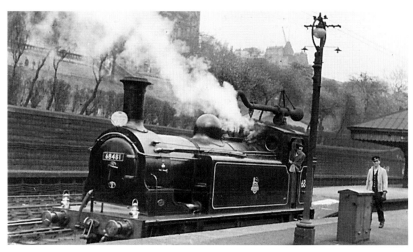

At Edinburgh Waverley there used to be a station pilot engine in immaculate livery (lined black). It seems to have been the custom to keep the station pilots in this shining condition, as was done at Liverpool Street with the N7 and J69 locomotives. This is J83 0-6-0T number 68481 at Waverley on 6th May 1957. The designer was M. Holmes, and the first of thirty-nine commenced work in 1900.

The largest class of locomotives was the GWR's pannier tank, which, in various forms, totalled 1226 between 1901 and 1956, when the last 9400 class were produced by Swindon. There were eight principal classes, and an example is shown of the 5700 class, which alone had 863 representatives. Number 7782 is at Maiden Newton on 10th October 1962, taking the 17.18 to Bridport. The GWR green gave place to black in their later years.

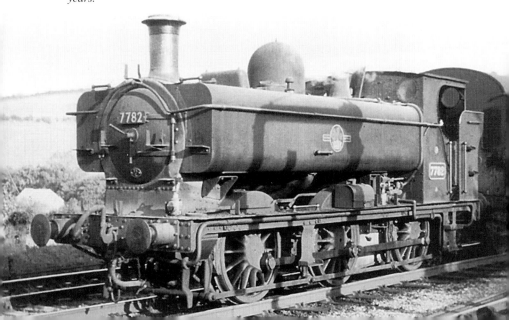

and freight trains. In the 1930s they took over the Broad Street to Hatfield services, previously entrusted to the Adams 4-4-0Ts of the North London Railway. These 0-6-0Ts, or Jinties as they were called, stood any amount of thrashing that was necessary if their 4 foot 7 inch (1397 mm) wheels were to develop enough speed to keep time. In 1909 H. Wainwright decided that an engine something like the Brighton Terrier would be useful for the South Eastern & Chatham Railway, and he brought out the little P class, but only a few were constructed. However, several examples survive.

But the outstanding 0-6-0T design came from Swindon, at first as a saddle tank, and later and in much greater numbers as a pannier tank. There were ten variations between 1897 and 1956, when they were still being turned out by Swindon, and the total number was well over twelve hundred. These capable engines were used for shunting and short-haul freight trains, but they had a monopoly of certain branches such as Bridport and Fairford and above all were used on the numerous Welsh valley lines. In their last years they went beyond their normal frontiers and were to be found shunting and working empty stock at Clapham Junction, banking on the Lickey Incline and to The Mound and Helmsdale in the far north. This ubiquity was a great tribute to the soundness of their design.

A favourite wheel arrangement for passenger tank engines in the nineteenth century was the 0-4-4, and at least twelve companies made use of them. Survivors are Adams's O2 on the LSWR, once to be found on any country branch and later settling in the Isle of Wight; they enjoyed longevity since they dated from 1889. In 1897 Drummond turned out the M7 from Eastleigh, having the usual sturdy features and a turn for speed. The heavy front end may have caused the derailment at Tavistock in 1898 and again at Raynes Park in 1933, although the criticism should be directed to the track rather than to the locomotive. Urie added his superheater to number 126, but this made a heavy engine even heavier, and the apparatus was not fitted to any other. However, the class did a vast amount of suburban work very satisfactorily for many years until electrification made them redundant. Another very useful design was that of H. Wainwright in 1904, working on the SECR on London and country branch duties at first, but later in their lives appearing on various parts of the Southern Region.

One of the most handsome types to run on British rails was Adams's 4-4-2T of 1882, the Radial. In their youth they were ubiquitous, but towards the end of their working days they had a liking for Dorset and could be seen on the Lyme Regis branch. In 1904 there was an awareness in the board rooms of the railways that competition was arising from the growing road traffic. This resulted in the various works pro-

The year 1889 saw the first of William Adams's O2 class 0-4-4T, introduced for light duty. They were pretty little engines and were improved by Drummond's flared chimney to replace the Adams 'coffee pot' type. In all there were sixty, and twenty-three survived to be taken over by BR. Their latter days were spent in the Isle of Wight, as is shown by number W14 'Fishbourne' with a Ventnor train at Ryde St John's Road on 29th April 1965. This was the 14.45 from Ryde Pier Head. The lined black finish suited them well.

The LSWR had another type of 0-4-4T in Drummond's massive M7 class. The first began to work on suburban trains in 1897, and they proved so useful that the total number produced was 105, of which 103 were handed over to BR on 1st January 1948. Number 30055 is taking water at Three Bridges on 22nd March 1961 before departing with the 14.25 train to East Grinstead. The LSWR green finish gave place to lined black under nationalisation.

Most of the pre-grouping railways used the 0-4-4T engine and H. Wainwright produced his version in 1904. The H class ran to sixty-six locomotives, and sixty-four were taken over by BR. They were seen all over the SECR; number 31263 is shown pausing at Horsmonden with the 12.30 train from Paddock Wood to Hawkhurst on 13th April 1961. The engines were painted green originally, but the normal lined-out black after 1947.

ducing steam rail-motors. Sometimes the engine unit formed one bogie of a coach with a normal bogie at the other end. These rail-motors were adopted widely, but as the power of a steam bogie was limited many railways chose to have a normal tank engine permanently coupled to two or more coaches. The locomotive remained at one end of the train or was sometimes placed in the middle, and the driver operated controls at each end of the train, the coach ends being fitted with large windows. The fireman remained on the engine. On the Great Western a handy 0-4-2T was developed, coupled to one end of the train, and these could be

In 1882 William Adams brought out what must be one of the most graceful locomotives ever built. This was his Radial 4-4-2T, of which seventy-one were built. They looked even better when Drummond replaced the plain Adams chimney with his own more slender type. This is a view of number 30582 at Axminster on 3rd May 1958 ready to haul the 12.33 to Lyme Regis. The last coach of the London train can be seen. Green in LSWR days, they spent their last years in black, lined out.

In 1898 a new 4-4-2T engine appeared on the Great Northern Railway, built to the designs of H. A. Ivatt. These locomotives took over the work of the older Stirling 0-4-4Ts. A most useful class, they numbered fifty in all and were to be seen all over the LNER system, designated C12. The last was scrapped in 1959. The BR finish was lined black, but in their early days they were green. The photograph, taken on 29th June 1954, shows number 67380 (formerly 1527) ready to leave Seaton Junction (Rutland) for Peterborough.

seen from 1932 or thereabouts all over the system.

For many years towards the end of the nineteenth century the Great Eastern Railway, under the guidance first of W. Worsdell and then of J. Holden, could not make up its mind whether the 0-4-4T or the 2-4-2T was the better proposition for suburban working. In 1915 A. J. Hill settled the question in a most capable manner by introducing his powerful 0-6-2T (LNER N7). These engines played with the light rolling stock which made up the Liverpool Street suburban trains, and they appealed to Gresley so much that he had a large number built. Construction went on under Thompson until 1943, and the later ones had round-topped fireboxes to conform with Doncaster usage. Their rivals on the Great Northern were Gresley's own N2 0-6-2Ts, the first imposing example appearing in 1920. They continued to appear until 1925. The N7 was more powerful than the N2, but the latter was faster. Nevertheless, Great Northern drivers tended to prefer the Great Eastern type, as their own N2, with its high-pitched boiler, could develop 'hunting' at speed. The N2 also had generous lead in the valve setting, and this could make starting difficult from the notorious platform 16 at King's Cross. During the latter part of the 1930s Gresley lived at Salisbury Hall, near Potters Bar, and was in the habit of catching the 9.03 train to King's Cross. This train was always hauled by an N2 looking delightful in its livery of shining black paint.

The 1400 class 0-4-2T appeared on the GWR under Collett in 1932. Many were fitted for auto-train working. They numbered ninety-five, and here number 1470 is at Ashburton ready to leave with the 14.45 to Totnes on 7th May 1958. They were maintained in GWR Brunswick green.

LMR 2-4-2T number 50764 at Wakefield in 1949. This type was designed by Sir John Aspinall for the Lancashire & Yorkshire Railway in 1889. There were various rebuilds, the last being in 1935. It was a very successful type, being able to haul express trains between Liverpool and Manchester. They were later replaced by the Aspinall Atlantics and the Hughes 4-6-0s.

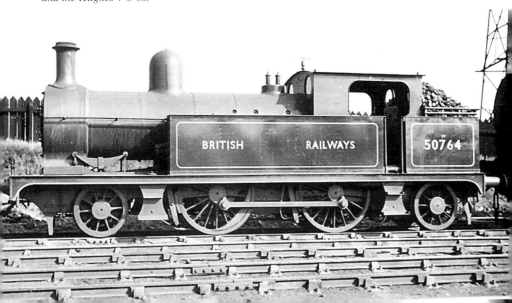

The E4 0-6-2T was built at Brighton Works in 1910 to the designs of D. Earle Marsh. They were useful on suburban traffic, and seventy-five appeared in batches with the names of places served by the London Brighton & South Coast Railway. Thus number 473 was called after 'Birch Grove', and it has been restored to its umber livery by the Bluebell Railway. It is shown at Sheffield Park after its renaming ceremony on 25th March 1962. Its BR number was 32473.

The numerous railways in the Welsh valleys were great users of the 0-6-2T engine. As they wore out, it was the policy of the GWR, which had absorbed the smaller lines from 1st January 1923, to bring out its own type. Thus we see number 6626 at Rhymney on a coal train on 27th April 1964. After the first one appeared in 1924 the family increased to two hundred.

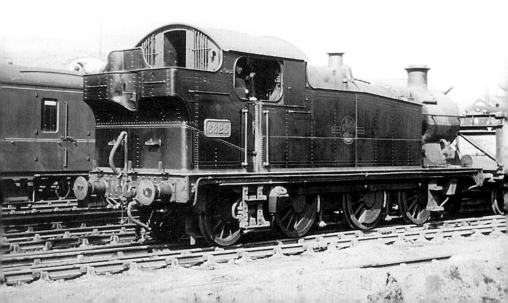

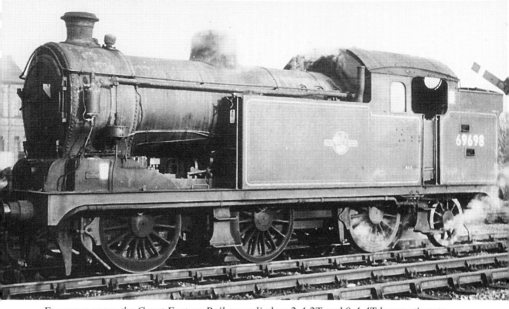

For many years the Great Eastern Railway relied on 2-4-2T and 0-4-4T locomotives to work their suburban services, but A. J. Hill, who became Locomotive Superintendent in 1912, resolved to improve services by designing a very powerful 0-6-2T. The first two were an immediate success in 1915, and Gresley later added to the numbers so that by 1943 there were 134 examples, but most with round-topped Doncaster fireboxes. The picture is of number 69698 (class N7) on freight work at Luton (Bute Street) on 25th January 1961. The finish was lined black.

The increase in suburban traffic after the First World War necessitated the use of a locomotive more powerful than the C12 4-4-2T and N1 0-6-2T. Gresley therefore introduced the excellent N2 0-6-2T in 1920, and it showed great power on the High Barnet branch and attained 60 mph (96 km/h) on the Hatfield service. The class increased until there were 107, and several had condensing apparatus fitted for working the trains to Moorgate. Number 69535 is being prepared for duty at King's Cross on 14th October 1961.

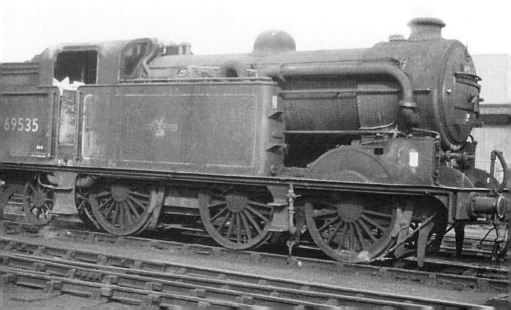

The South Wales coal traffic had always formed an important part of GWR income, and the long haul of coal trains was performed by the 2800 class of 2-8-0 tender engines. For the short haul, and the marshalling of heavy coal trains near Severn Tunnel Junction, Churchward turned out a 2-8-0T engine in 1910. Collett built more in 1923, and they had the GWR green livery. Number 4258 was standing at Old Oak Common in 1938 when the photograph was taken. The class numbered 151.

In order to obtain longer haulage distances Collett decided to enlarge the coal bunker of the 4200 class and so produced the 7200 2-8-2T class in 1934. Number 7252 is seen at the head of a heavy coal train leaving Westbury on 28th April 1952. Rear assistance is being given by an 0-6-2T engine.

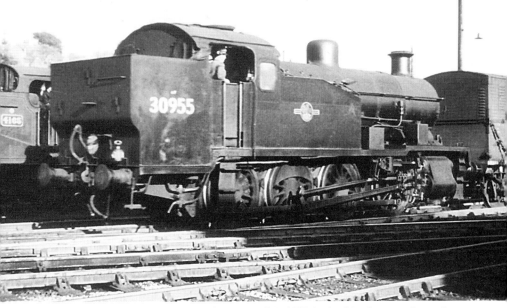

The class Z 0-8-0T was brought out by Maunsell in 1929 for banking heavy trains and shunting in the London marshalling yards. One unexpected tribute came from residents in the London suburbs who slept better through the soft 'woof-woof-woof' of the three-cylinder engine, as compared with the sharp bark of the two-cylinder. Here number 30955 is helping at the rear of a Southern Region train climbing from Exeter St David's to Central on 8th May 1961. First in green and later in black, they numbered only eight.

The favourite engine on the smaller Welsh railways before 1923 was the 0-6-2T, and these were taken over by the Great Western during the latter part of the year. As they wore out, despite rebuilding at Swindon, Collett decided to replace them with his own version, and the first of the 5600 class of 0-6-2T began working in 1924. For heavy coal traffic, when the journey was short, Churchward had brought out a 2-8-0T in 1910, and these were multiplied by Collett. An engine with greater capacity in its coal bunkers was desirable, and this prompted Collett to put on the road a 2-8-2T engine. These very impressive-looking engines used to perform banking duties at Llanvihangel and elsewhere. Large freight tank engines also came from Eastleigh, where Urie had put to work some 4-6-2Ts and, for the hump yard at Feltham, there was a 4-8-0T variety. These fine machines commenced duties in 1921.

Over the years there has been nothing to beat the 2-6-2T type for inner suburban duty and the 2-6-4T for outer suburban and main line. To Churchward must go the credit for having initiated this kind of locomotive, for in 1906 he made the prototype for what became, in later years, the 4500 class. There was an earlier class of 2-6-2T as Hoy, of the Lancashire & Yorkshire Railway, had produced twenty in 1903. They were, however, of a different, rather rigid type and do not invalidate Churchward's claim to be the originator of the modern type. The Great Western engines were small and designed to work on country

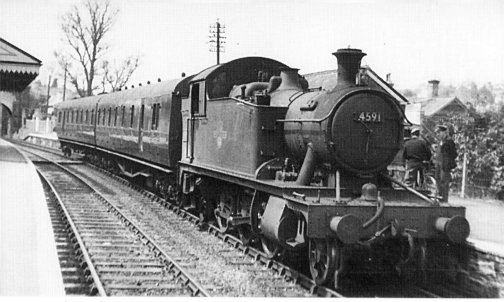

Some of Dean's tank engines for the GWR were not conspicuously successful, and Churchward made a great step forward when he designed a standard 2-6-2T locomotive. The 4500 class was seen mostly on country branches from 1906, and Collett added others in 1927. The picture shows a typical GWR country scene with number 4591 at Launceston on 9th May 1958 ready to take the 12.50 (Saturdays only) train to Plymouth. This class reached a total of 148, finished in the normal GWR green.

J. G. Robinson, Chief Mechanical Engineer of the Great Central Railway, had brought out a very useful heavy freight engine in 1902. After forty years they were due for withdrawal, but Edward Thompson, CME of the LNER, decided to rebuild them as shunting engines. They thus became 0-8-0T locomotives and were produced with a great saving of steel, a matter of paramount importance during the Second World War. Number 69929 is shown here at Langwith Junction on 23rd March 1958. The class lasted twenty years after their introduction in 1942.

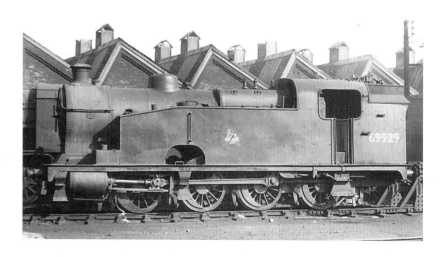

branches. His larger engine was of 4-4-2T layout but was more a synthesis of standard parts than a newly designed type. Collett did better with a 2-6-2T with larger driving wheels than those of the 4500 and turned out from Swindon a very useful and fast engine in the 3100, 4100, 5100, 6100 and 8100 groups. Fowler had presided over a 2-6-2T to relieve the aged Kirtley and Johnson 0-4-4Ts, and although they had the necessary adhesion they were sluggish on the main line. They appeared from Derby in 1930, which was the year in which Gresley designed the excellent V1 type, to be followed by the more powerful V3 in 1939. These three-cylinder 2-6-2Ts were most capable but were rarely seen in London. Their home was in Scotland. In contrast with his 2-6-2Ts, Fowler produced a 2-6-4T engine in 1927 that had tremendous capabilities. They were good on outer suburban work and came into their own during the Second World War when they were easily able to take over an express train if the locomotive had failed. Other 2-6-2T designs were Stanier's class 3 for the LMS in 1935, which used to get short of breath, and Ivatt's supremely successful class 2 of 1946. The 84000 engine made by various works under Riddles was based on the Ivatt design, while the class 3 was a new departure with a Swindon number 4 boiler. They did a good deal of country work but also acted as station pilots at Waterloo and other termini. These were numbered 82000 onwards.

Swindon had produced a larger version of the 2-6-2T in 1903, and again Collett brought out more with modifications. Of those built between 1928 and 1931, the photograph depicts number 6163 on shunting duties at Oxford on 1st August 1959. This useful and speedy type reached a total of 238 in the GWR Brunswick green with copper-topped chimney.

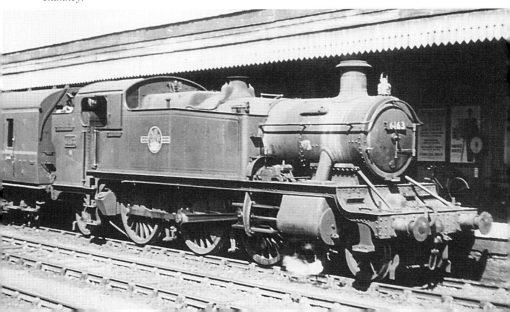

The London Midland & Scottish Railway also used the 2-6-2T type for local services, and H. G. Ivatt scored a great success with the willing little class 2 design. Number 41222 is wearing its first BR livery of lined-out black and 'British Railways' on the tank and is seen at Willesden in 1949. The first of the class, number 1200, appeared in 1946, and there were 130 of them.

Turning now to the 2-6-4T wheel arrangement, it is pleasant to record that Maunsell was able to return to this type in 1931 after his great misfortune with the K class in 1927. His W class 2-6-4T was a powerful three-cylinder engine introduced specially for heavy freight working in

The British Rail Standard class 2 2-6-2T was very similar to Ivatt's for the LMSR. In the same livery, they started life in 1953, and thirty were produced. Number 84004 has just arrived at Newport Pagnell with the 14.45 from Wolverton on 1st August 1959.

The BR class 3 2-6-2T was a new departure, and forty-five appeared after 1952. Some were used as station pilots at Waterloo, but most were to be found on country branches. Number 82019 has just left Halwill Junction with the 1654 to Bude on 9th May 1958. Note the excellent design of bunker.

the London suburbs and on the continual north to south traffic (and vice versa) that is carried on daily but inconspicuously. Being heavy workhorses, they had not quite the elegance of the K and K1 classes but were

The 2-6-4T type of locomotive was very popular in Britain. After Maunsell had converted his K and K1 classes to 2-6-0 tender engines, he returned to the type in 1931 with the powerful W class, of which fifteen were built. They had three cylinders and were ideal for working heavy freight trains to and from the northern lines. This is a view of number 31918 at Clapham Junction on 17th July 1962. Freight engines were painted plain black.

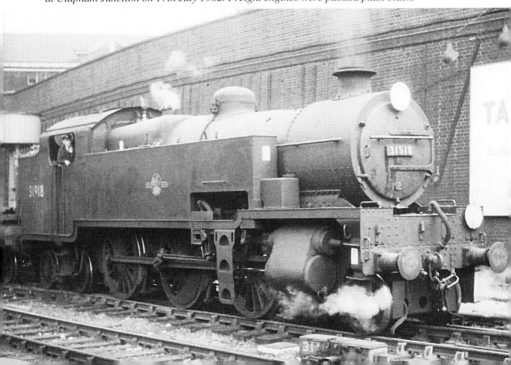

good-looking. Strangely, they had three separate sets of Walschaerts valve gear, and not two with derived motion, as invented by Maunsell's assistant, Holcroft. This was used, however, on the three-cylinder tank engine number A890. Some speculation has arisen about Stanier's decision to build a three-cylinder 2-6-4T engine in 1934, but it is thought that Gresley's successful 2-6-2T of 1930 may have influenced him. This rather unnecessary locomotive did good work on the London Tilbury & Southend Railway, but Stanier's two-cylinder counterpart numbered from 2425, dating from 1935, was every bit as good as the three-cylinder type and less complicated. They were in effect a taper boiler example of Fowler's 1930 engine. In 1945 Fairburn continued the Stanier two-cylinder locomotive but used a shorter wheelbase and saved 2 tons in weight.

The last 2-6-4T built for the old companies was Thompson's L1 class. This could be described as the result of over-standardisation, seeing that it included the same cylinders, driving wheels and boiler pressure as the K1 2-6-0. These features resulted in an enormously powerful tank engine with a tractive effort of over 32,000 pounds (14,500 kg), and during BR days some of the type were given cylinders of reduced diameter and lower boiler pressure. However, they must have been a

Under Sir Henry Fowler a very modern type of 2-6-4T engine was designed at Derby in 1927, and they not only ran the fast suburban trains but took over heavy expresses during the Second World War. They numbered 125 in all, and number 42338 has just buffered up to a train of empty stock at St Pancras on 12th October 1961. The livery was lined black.

In 1934 thirty-seven three-cylinder 2-6-4T locomotives were designed by Stanier to work trains on the London Tilbury & Southend section. The 4-4-2T engines that had worked the thirteen-coach trains so successfully were beginning to show signs of age. The engine crews preferred the two-cylinder 2-6-4Ts, which were also supplied from Crewe. Number 42516 is hauling a wagon of litter at Fenchurch Street station on 9th February 1961. The finish of these engines was in the normal lined black.

Sir William Stanier was succeeded by C. E. Fairburn as Chief Mechanical Engineer, and the latter modified the successful two-cylinder 2-6-4T and achieved a saving of 2 tons in weight. Fairburn engine number 42132 waits at Southport Chapel Street station to take the 8.40 to Preston on 3rd May 1965. The total number was very large – 206 of Stanier's and 277 of Fairburn's, 483 in all. They had the usual lined black finish and first appeared in 1935.

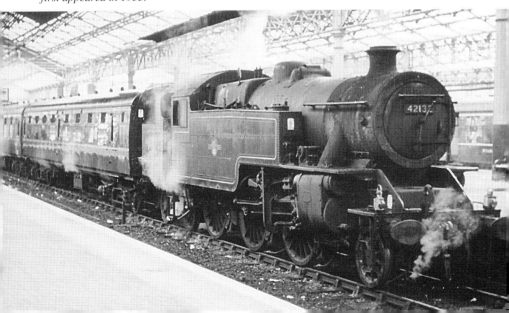

most useful family of locomotives for no fewer than ninety-nine were
built by Peppercorn, who succeeded Thompson, and construction went
on until 1950. Travellers between Princes Risborough or Aylesbury
and Marylebone took note of their excellent accelerative powers and
their capacity for high speed. The corresponding BR Standard class
was numbered from 80000 and rated class 4. They were as good as
Stanier's engines but had a slightly lower water capacity in their tanks.
This gave rise to an unfounded report that they were heavier on water
than the LMS type. What occurred was nothing more than a slightly
lower water level in the tank at the end of a journey. The first engine
took the road in 1951

An interesting variation on the tank engine theme was put forward by
Vincent Raven in 1913 in the form of his 4-4-4T design. These were
very handsome engines but limited to the adhesion of four-coupled
wheels. In 1931 Gresley rebuilt these as 4-6-2Ts, and these three-cylinder machines were able to do wonderful work on the heavy inclines to
be found in the area of Pickering, Whitby, Scarborough and Middles-
brough. It was only in 1960, forty-seven years after their first emer-
gence, that these engines were withdrawn.

The LNER variant of the 2-6-4T was constructed at Doncaster in 1945 to the design of
Edward Thompson. At Cambridge, number 67720 is seen acting as station pilot on 15th
April 1960. Although Thompson was in office only long enough to see his prototype
launched, his successor, A. H. Peppercorn, had another ninety-nine built in 1946 to
1948, so that they must have been very satisfactory. They were turned out in lined black.

In 1951 BR put on the road a 2-6-4T engine in which Riddles followed the example set by Stanier sixteen years before. They looked well in the polished lined black, and 155 were constructed at various works. Quite late in the days of steam they worked the Victoria-Oxted-East Grinstead service, and the picture is of 80144 taking water at Oxted at the head of the 14.09 from Victoria on 2nd November 1961. They had the excellent unobstructed view from the rear spectacles like other BR designs and the LNER L1s.

In 1911 J. G. Robinson introduced a powerful 4-6-2T engine for working outer surburban trains. They were so successful that Gresley built more in 1925. They were called 'Coronation' tanks as 1911 was the year of the coronation of King George V. Classed as A5/1 and A5/2, this excellent Great Central design lasted until 1961. Number 69804 is seen at Langwith Junction in 1955.

Freight locomotives

Until the end of the Second World War the basic income of all the great railways had been from the transport of freight, particularly coal. Such companies as the Great Western, the London & North Western, the Midland, the Great Northern and later the Great Central derived enormous revenues from their coal trains. The traffic was so much sought after that it could be said that where there was a Midland branch to a colliery there would also be one from the Great Central, lying parallel. Passenger traffic brought in an income, but the cost of operation was much greater, and the heavily loaded trains to coastal resorts ran only during the summer. A chief mechanical engineer would therefore make sure that he designed a competent goods or freight engine, and in the nineteenth century it was customary to use the 0-6-0 type almost exclusively, the heavier 0-8-0 and 2-8-0 becoming essential as the trains grew longer. The Great Eastern, having little coal traffic, used light 0-6-0 locomotives which could go all over the system without restriction. Such was the celebrated Y14 (LNER J15) class. These useful power units began life in 1883 and did not disappear until the last days of steam. Number 930 was famous because in 1891 the engine and tender had been built in nine and three quarter hours, duly painted in workshop grey, and soon afterwards it was in steam. All the parts had

One of the goods types with the greatest longevity must surely have been T. W. Worsdell's 0-6-0 dating from 1883. Known as LNER J15 (Y14 on the Great Eastern), they could go anywhere and so numbered 289. The view is of number 7847 (65366) shunting at Broxbourne in 1935. They were finished in plain black.

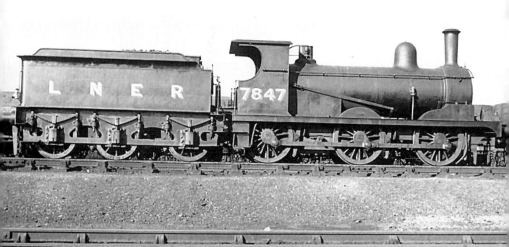

The Midland Railway had four classes of 0-6-0 designated Classes 1, 2, 3 and 4. Class 1 denoted Kirtley outside frame engines, and these were followed by S. W Johnson's design (Class 2) of 1875. Extensive rebuilding was carried out in 1917 and subsequent years. Belpaire fireboxes were fitted. These engines were ideal for such branches as Kettering to Huntingdon. The photograph above shows number 58283 at Walsall in 1957.

As they were not required to operate at continual high speeds like the express passenger engine, goods engines, or freight as they are now termed, tended to have long lives. Midland class 3 0-6-0 locomotives originated in 1885-96, and large numbers of the 482 built remained to the end of steam. Number 43248 is taking the 14.20 train from Highbridge to Evercreech Junction and is seen pausing at Glastonbury on 3rd May 1958. Freight engines were in unlined black.

been machined and laid out in the erecting shop, but the work of assembling and constructing the locomotive set a record which has never been beaten.

The inside cylinder 0-6-0 was the accepted type at this time for goods work, just as the inside cylinder 4-4-0 was the standard express engine. Other companies had well-known examples, such as the Midland class 3 (1885), the North Eastern class C (LNER J21), the LNWR Cauliflower and the LSWR 700 class. The LNWR engine got its name from the company's coat of arms, which was painted on the driving-wheel splasher. The North Eastern Railway's C class (J21) had been designed by T. W. Worsdell in 1886 and F. W. Webb's Cauliflower in the following year. At this period of locomotive development the need was for a medium-sized engine that could operate all over the system and, if need be, take a hand with excursion traffic. This type is represented by Holmes's 0-6-0 dating from 1888 and by the Caledonian example of 1899, designed by J. F. McIntosh and later rated as class 3 by the London Midland & Scottish Railway. In the south, Wainwright had brought out his class C in 1900 with the usual handsome outline, and in 1908 D. Earle Marsh designed the class C for the London Brighton & South Coast Railway, later to be rebuilt and named C2x. Some had a second dome for experiments in feed-water heating, and when the possibilities had been fully explored and then abandoned the apparatus was removed, but the second dome remained.

As coal traffic originated principally in the north of England it is not surprising to find the North Eastern Railway again improving its fleet of 0-6-0 engines by the P2 (LNER J26) of 1906, a W. Worsdell design. In 1921 Sir Vincent Raven went still further with the P3 class (LNER

Holmes's sturdy 0-6-0 (LNER J36) dated from 1888 and number 65288 is at Haymarket, Edinburgh, on 7th May 1963 ready for the day's work. The total number was 168 in the usual black, but they were fitted with vacuum or vacuum plus Westinghouse brakes for passenger-train working as required.

On the South Eastern & Chatham Railway H. Wainwright always designed an engine with handsome lines. His C 0-6-0 class originated in 1900, and 109 were built at Ashford, of which ninety-two passed to BR. Near the end of their lives some became departmental locomotives, and DS239 is at Ashford on 6th August 1964 on shunting duties. The finish was plain black.

The locomotive depot at Three Bridges always had an interesting collection of steam engines, such as number 32438 of the C2x class dating from 1908. These 0-6-0 engines originated under R. J. Billinton, but others were built under D. Earle Marsh ('x' means rebuilt on the London Brighton & South Coast Railway). The photograph was taken on 7th December 1961, and all fifty-five of these engines ended their careers in black. Some had an additional dome to accommodate a top feed experiment, but when the apparatus was removed the extra dome remained.

J27), which looked most impressive with its boiler 5 feet 6 inches (1676 mm) in diameter. If the Gresley J6 of 1911 could be described as rather more suited to mixed traffic than freight, the same cannot be said of the S. D. Holden engine of 1912, which was purely a goods creation. These had Belpaire fireboxes, which were replaced by the round-topped type in 1934 when they were rebuilt by Gresley. In 1920 the Great Eastern Railway achieved fame by A. J. Hill's enormous 0-6-0 (LNER J20), which by its tractive effort of 29,000 pounds (13,000 kg) became the most powerful engine of this wheel arrangement in Great Britain. This distinction lasted until 1942, when Bulleid's Q1 took first place. The J20 class was rebuilt by Thompson in 1943 with the Doncaster type of boiler replacing the Belpaire, and they continued on heavy duty work until 1962.

On other railways there had been similar progress. The coal trains on the Midland Railway were becoming heavier, and each had to be hauled by two class 3 0-6-0s, a wasteful procedure. After 1918 some unusual combinations of locomotives were seen on coal trains between Toton and Brent, for example a class 3 0-6-0 piloted by a Johnson 4-2-2 or Spinner. Or a Kirtley outside frames 2-4-0 would assist one of

In order to supplement his J6 class 0-6-0, dating from 1911, Gresley put on the road his powerful J39 class in 1926. They worked all over the LNER system and numbered 289 in all. They were in the normal black and had a 4200 gallon tender. They were, however, 8 tons heavier than the J6, and this gave them a route availability of only 6 (RA6). Number 64888 is ready to leave Langholm on 8th April 1959 with the 10.42 train to Riddings Junction and Carlisle.

The Midland Railway had 0-6-0 types of classes 2, 3 and 4. The last appeared during the reign of Sir Henry Fowler in 1911, but more came out in 1924 and 1941. They could be seen on excursion passenger trains as well as freight, and many had the vacuum break for the purpose. The total output was 770, in black. Number 44532 is at the head of a brick train from Elstow Works on 30th October 1961.

The heavy mineral traffic on the former Midland main line had required trains to be double-headed for some years. In 1927 Sir Henry Fowler supervised the construction of the mammoth Garratt 2-6-0, 0-6-2 engines. The tractive effort was 45,620 pounds, and the weight 155 tons. After the trial of the first three, thirty more appeared in 1933. These had rotating coal bunkers to assist the fireman. They gave a sterling performance with trains up to 1000 tons. Unfortunately none has been preserved. The picture shows number 47969 working hard with a train of iron ore, negotiating the sharp uphill curve at Wellingborough. This curve connected the former LNWR line with the Midland main line.

Whitelegg's beautiful 4-6-4T engines, newly acquired from the London Tilbury & Southend Railway. To rectify this state of affairs, Fowler brought out the well-known 4F 0-6-0, which was extensively produced. They had a healthy 'Derby roar' when working hard and were big enough in the wheel to deal with excursion trains. The first took the road in 1911. The Toton to Brent run from 1927 to 1956 was in the hands of thirty-three massive 2-6-0, 0-6-2 Garratts made by Beyer Peacock & Co Ltd. Three had been tried initially, and the remaining thirty supplied as soon as the performance of the first was found to be satisfactory. They could pull fifty loaded wagons of coal and eighty empties. In the view of the enginemen these locomotives were hard work for the fireman, gave the driver plenty of hauling and brake power (very important) and both a comfortable ride. While speaking of Garratt engines, the greatest of them all must be mentioned. This was Gresley's mammoth 2-8-0, 0-8-2 six-cylinder banking engine, which commenced work at Wath in 1925. It was really two of Gresley's O2 2-8-0 engines on one chassis with a very large boiler in the centre. In LNER days it bore the number 2395 but finished its days as 69999.

But, returning to the 0-6-0 engines, there were many different designs, and it is possible to mention only the more important ones. In

Maunsell's last design for the Southern Railway was the Q 0-6-0, dating from 1938. It is said that they were based on the Midland 4F 0-6-0, and they were powerful machines but lacked sufficient braking power for heavy freight work. Only twenty were made, painted in plain black, and some retained the steam reversing gear. Bulleid gave them all a multiple-jet exhaust with wide chimney, and number 30540 is seen thus at Three Bridges on 7th December 1961.

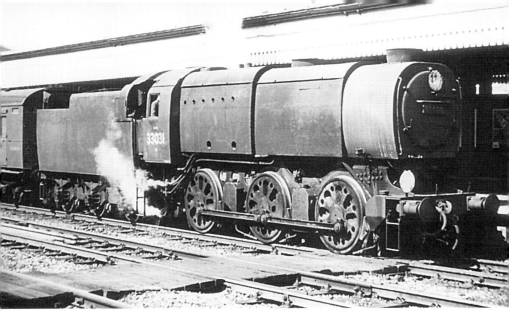

O. V. Bulleid was very busy with his Merchant Navy class during the Second World War but found time to design the unusual-looking Q1 0-6-0 in 1942. Although their appearance caused a good deal of comment they did well on freight work and had a most surprising turn of speed when hauling passenger trains. Forty were constructed, and number 33031 has just arrived at Ashford with a parcels train. The date is 30th April 1960. They had the usual freight livery.

1883 Dean had brought out his famous goods engine, which lasted until 1957, but as they wore out Collett decided to replace them with a design of his own, the 2200 class. The first emerged from Swindon in 1930 and they showed themselves as useful on passenger work as they were on pick-up freight. They could be seen all over the Great Western – on stopping trains between Banbury and Oxford, on the former Cambrian Railways – and later on they took turns with LMS and BR Standard types on the Somerset & Dorset Joint Railway. Their well-designed cylinders, ports and valve gear made them speedy, although a short wheelbase 0-6-0 could give a rough ride on the footplate when express speeds were attained. The long list of 0-6-0 types is not yet exhausted, although new designs became rarer in the 1930s. In 1938 Maunsell brought out his last type of locomotive, and this was based on his admiration for the London Midland & Scottish 4F 0-6-0. His Q class certainly resembled the 4F, and according to footplate men it did very well on passenger trains and light goods trains. For heavy loose-coupled freight, however, it proved to be rather weak in brake power. Finally we come to a much discussed locomotive that caused a great deal of comment, favourable and otherwise, when it appeared in 1942. That extremely able engineer O. V. Bulleid naturally wished to see as many of his designs take shape as possible, but during the Second World War the government did not encourage the use of materials unnecessarily.

But Bulleid obtained permission to build his Q1 provided he econo-
mised in steel, and he certainly did so. The Q1 was the most unusual-
looking engine to take the rails since Paget's 2-6-2 of 1908. But the Q1
was an excellent machine and was as surefooted on goods work as it
was fast on passenger.

At the end of the nineteenth century and the beginning of the twentieth there was a change in express locomotive design from four-coupled
to six-coupled, and in the case of freight engines from six to eight.
Francis Webb had continued his compounding by designing a three-
cylinder compound 0-8-0 in 1893 and a four-cylinder type in 1901.
However, between 1903 and 1909 George Whale rebuilt most of them
as simple engines and converted some to the 2-8-0 wheel arrangement,
but the modern type was originated by Bowen-Cooke, who in 1912
introduced an efficient superheated 0-8-0 called class G, although the
crews always called them 'Super Ds'. The Lancashire & Yorkshire
joined the ranks of the 0-8-0 users in 1900 with Aspinall's example,
followed in 1901 by McIntosh on the Caledonian and Ivatt on the Great
Northern, in this case the locomotives being known as 'Long Toms'.
Always to the fore with powerful types, J. G. Robinson on the Great
Central used outside cylinders in 1902, whereas Hughes, on the Lancashire & Yorkshire, kept to inside cylinders in his 1910 version. A most
impressive design with outside cylinders came from Vincent Raven on

The London & North Western's best freight engine was the G2a 0-8-0, of which 273
were built from 1917 onwards. They were found all over the system, and number 49114
is shown at Ryecroft Junction. They were sometimes seen at Cambridge on passenger
work when traffic was heavy in the summer. It is not surprising that such a useful type
should have lasted until 1964. Fortunately number 9395 has been preserved.

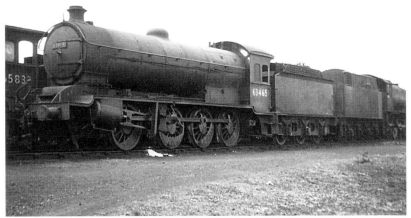

After his work during the First World War for the government, Sir Vincent Raven returned to the North Eastern Railway, and in 1919 he designed the remarkable three-cylinder T3 (LNER Q7). One was sent to the 1921 Glenfarg trials, which required the engine to haul a heavy freight train up 6¹/₂ miles at 1 in 74. Number 903 actually performed the best, the others being a GWR 2-8-0 and a North British 0-6-0. Only fifteen were constructed, in their later years in black, and number 63465 (624) is shown at Darlington shed on 5th May 1960.

the North Eastern in 1913. These were known as class T1 and T2 and survived until 1967. The most famous Darlington engine was the three cylinder T3 (LNER Q7), which started work in 1919. It proved to be equal to any task set for it, and it was number 903 of this class that took part in the Glenfarg trials on the North British Railway in 1921. The Glenfarg bank lies on the route between Perth and Edinburgh, and a contest was held between a North British J37 0-6-0, a North Eastern T3 0-8-0 and a Great Western 2-8-0. The larger engines naturally did better, the GWR number 2804 taking a 590-ton train quite easily. How-

The North Eastern Railway, which became a constituent of the London & North Eastern Railway in 1923, throve principally on its freight traffic. For heavy coal trains Sir Vincent Raven designed the T2 0-8-0 (LNER Q6), and these performed wonderful work from 1913 onwards. The photograph shows number 63410 at Hartlepool in 1955. The last one was withdrawn in 1967, but fortunately number 3395 has been preserved.

ever, on another day, with 680 tons the engine slipped and stalled owing
to the gravity sanding being ineffective in a snowstorm. This was no
criticism of the engine design: in fact, the GWR adherence to gravity
sanding was troublesome for engine number 5000 *Launceston Castle*
when climbing to Shap in wet weather in 1926. Later, in good weather,
the NER engine number 903 took 750 tons up to Glenfarg without
difficulty. The last 0-8-0 design was by Fowler in 1929, a most impressive locomotive, of which 175 examples were constructed.

The 2-8-0 evolved naturally from the 0-8-0 as it gave a better riding
vehicle, permitted a longer boiler and had the pony truck to support any
additional weight that three cylinders might necessitate. The first in the
field was the Great Western's 2800 class, which Churchward produced
early in his career as Chief Mechanical Engineer. Like so many Swindon products the 2800 class was a success from the beginning. They
were particularly valuable on the long trains of Welsh coal that had to
descend into and climb out of the Severn Tunnel. Collett continued to
add to their numbers right up to 1938. In 1911 J. G. Robinson of the
Great Central Railway designed a 2-8-0 that became famous. They
were solidly built, as was customary at Gorton, and did so well that they
attracted the attention of the government during the First World War
and were chosen as the standard type for military purposes in Great
Britain and at any theatre of war overseas. Ninety-one were sent abroad,
and after the war the Great Western took fifty into stock, and gradually
supplied them with Swindon boiler accessories. The London & North
Eastern had as many as 413, which is not surprising as the Great Central
formed part of the LNER. During the Second World War the chief

Great Western Railway 2-8-0 number 3822 at Didcot (GWR Society) on 31st May 1988.
This type was introduced by G. J. Churchward in 1903 and multiplied by C. B. Collett in
1938. They totalled 167 engines, the last being withdrawn in 1966.

Persuaded by the success of Raven's three-cylinder engines, Gresley decided to adopt the same measures for his larger engines. In 1918 he altered a two-cylinder 2-8-0, number 461, to three cylinders with derived motion for the inside valve. The O2 class was developed from this with improved gear. Sixty-seven locomotives with three cylinders were built at Doncaster up to 1932, finished in plain black. Number 63986 is the leading engine in this impressive display of motive power. The giants are respectively O2/3, Robinson O2/4 and again Gresley O2/2, all returning to depot at Worksop on 17th August 1961.

mechanical engineers of the four groups had to contend with run-down locomotives and worn-out track, so that emphasis had to be laid on rebuilding existing designs rather than bringing out entirely new types. On the London & North Eastern, where money had never been plentiful, Thompson decided to rebuild the strong but obsolescent Robinson 2-8-0 engines, and some were given new 100A boilers, but others not only had new boilers but also entirely new cylinders with modern valve motion and steam passages. The latter rebuilds were designated class O1, and in the 1948 trials they made themselves conspicuous by showing the best coal consumption figures, namely 3.37 pounds per drawbar horsepower-hour. This performance must have given Thompson great satisfaction although he had retired two years previously. The Midland Railway never went beyond the 0-6-0 for its own lines, but Derby produced a 2-8-0 in 1914 for the Somerset & Dorset Joint Railway, and these were ideal for the coal trains in the Midsomer Norton district, also taking their turn on passenger work during the summer months.

Railway enthusiasts living near the Great Northern Railway in 1918 would have heard an engine with an unfamiliar beat. This was number 461, a two-cylinder 2-8-0 which Gresley had fitted with three cylinders, the valves of the inside cylinder being worked by levers from the two

Thompson's tenure of office as CME of the LNER was marked by his decision to equip the railway with a stud of powerful standardised engines and thus make much needed economies. This often meant rebuilding existing types instead of designing new ones. For example he modernised many of the solid Robinson 2-8-0s, of which the LNER had 413. Of these he fitted fifty-seven with new cylinders and round-topped fireboxes, and two of them, numbers 63773 and 63789, did outstandingly well in the 1948 trials. Number 63873 of class O4/8, shown at Alford, had a new boiler but kept the original cylinders. The date is 18th September 1962, and the coal train is ready to move south.

outside. This rather ungainly valve motion was considerably improved after Gresley had discussed the matter with Harry Holcroft of the South Eastern & Chatham Railway. Subsequent locomotives had the well-known Gresley-Holcroft gear and were able to deal successfully with heavy coal trains. When the 2-8-0 type was developed into the P1 2-8-2

Derby sent some excellent 2-8-0 locomotives to the Somerset & Dorset Joint Railway in 1914, and all eleven were happy with either passenger or coal trains on the steep gradients. Number 53808 is here seen at Radstock on a train bound for Bath. The last was withdrawn in 1964.

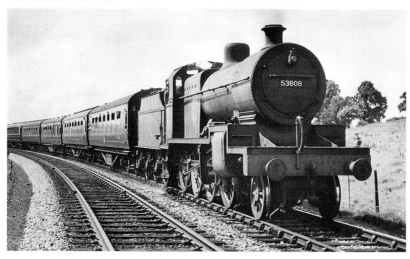

Stanier's successful 8F 2-8-0 class were seen all over the LMSR. This is not surprising seeing that there were 773 of them. In the very last days of steam, three of them were kept at Blackpool North, and number 48646 is heading south through Preston on 23rd April 1968, its former shiny black looking dusty.

it was found that the trains brought south to Hornsey and Ferme Park were so long that the sidings could not accommodate them, and so these magnificent engines became more or less redundant. On the London Midland & Scottish Railway Stanier scored a great success with his 8F 2-8-0, which was manufactured in large numbers and was to be seen all over Britain. The first issued from Crewe in 1935 and its capabilities prompted the government to choose it for mass production for war service after 1939. This corresponded to what had been done in the 1914 war when the Robinson 2-8-0 was chosen. However, it was found that to make such a high-class machine took too many hours, and R. A. Riddles was authorised to bring out his Austerity 2-8-0 for the Ministry of Supply. The first engine appeared in 1943, and, although of simple design with round-topped firebox, it proved to be most effective and was popular with the engine crews. Such was the demand, both at home and overseas, that 935 were constructed and they became a familiar sight on Britain's railways.

The last freight locomotive to be considered is the celebrated class 9 2-10-0, which was designed by Riddles but appeared in 1954 after he had left the Railway Executive. 251 were turned out by various works, but it fell to Swindon to make the very last, number 92220, in lined green livery with copper-topped double chimney. It was named *Evening Star*. The haulage feats of these engines are well known, and the best description is given in *Mendip Engineman* by P. W. Smith, who both fired and drove these fine machines over the testing Somerset & Dorset Joint Railway

This brings to an end a brief description of the principal steam locomotive types that served on the railways of Britain between 1948 and 1968. The emphasis has been on those types which have been preserved and can therefore be seen in museums or on the many private preserved railways.

The concentration of all traffic on the railways between 1939 and 1945 resulted in a shortage of locomotives. R. A. Riddles, later CME of the British Transport Commission (Railway Executive), designed a simple but useful 2-8-0 for the Ministry of Supply. The total built was 935, of which 733 went to British Rail. The picture is of number 90516 on a train of empty wagons at Ashendon Junction on 5th January 1961.

Riddles's final design, which emerged from Crewe after he had left the BTC in 1954, was his best. Rated as class 9, these engines were not only powerful in the field of freight but achieved 90 mph (145 km/h) on passenger trains. This latter habit was officially repressed. There were 251 of these giants, and 2-10-0 number 92134 is toying with a load of sixty empty wagons near Millbrook (Bedfordshire) on 29th September 1961. The livery is black.

Places to visit

The museums and railways listed here are likely places to see former British Railways' steam locomotives. However, readers are advised to telephone before travelling to check opening times and dates and to ascertain what locomotives may be seen.

Avon Valley Railway, Bitton Station, Willsbridge, Bristol. Telephone: 0117-932 7296.
Battlefield Line, Shackerstone Station, Shackerstone, Market Bosworth, Leicestershire CV13 6NW. Telephone: 01827 880754.
Birmingham Museum of Science and Industry, Newhall Street, Birmingham B3 1RZ. Telephone: 0121-235 1661. (Temporarily closed; reopens in 2000.)
Birmingham Railway Museum, 670 Warwick Road, Tyseley, Birmingham B11 2HL. Telephone: 0121-707 4696.
Bluebell Railway, Sheffield Park Station, near Uckfield, East Sussex TN22 3QL. Telephone: 01825 723777; talking timetable 01825 722370.
Bodmin & Wenford Railway, Bodmin General Station, Bodmin, Cornwall PL31 1AQ. Telephone: 01208 73666.
Bo'ness & Kinneil Railway, The Station, Union Street, Bo'ness, West Lothian EH51 9AQ. Telephone: 01506 822298 or 822446.
Bowes Railway, Springwell Village, Gateshead, Tyne and Wear NE9 7QJ. Telephone: 0191-416 1847.
Bressingham Steam Museum, Bressingham, Diss, Norfolk IP22 2AB. Telephone: 01379 687386.
Buckinghamshire Railway Centre, Quainton Road Station, Quainton, Aylesbury, Buckinghamshire HP22 4BY. Telephone: 01296 655720; recorded message 01296 655450.
Cholsey & Wallingford Railway, St John's Road, Wallingford, Oxfordshire. Telephone: 01491 35067.
Colne Valley Railway, Castle Hedingham Station, Yeldham Road, Castle Hedingham, Halstead, Essex CO9 3DZ. Telephone: 01787 461174.
Darlington Railway Centre and Museum, North Road Station, Station Road, Darlington, County Durham DL3 6ST. Telephone: 01325 460532.
Dean Forest Railway, Norchard Steam Centre, Forest Road, New Mills, Lydney, Gloucestershire GL15 4ET. Telephone: 01594 845840; talking timetable 01594 843423.
Didcot Railway Centre, Didcot Station, Didcot, Oxfordshire OX11 7NJ. Telephone: 01235 817200.
East Anglian Railway Museum, Chappel & Wakes Colne Station, Chappel, Colchester, Essex CO6 2DS. Telephone: 01206 242524.
East Lancashire Railway, Bolton Street Station, Bury, Lancashire BL9 0EY. Telephone: 0161-705 5111 (weekdays) or 0161-764 7790 (weekends).
East Somerset Railway, Railway Station, Cranmore, Shepton Mallet, Somerset BA4 4QP. Telephone: 01749 880417.
Embsay & Bolton Abbey Steam Railway, The Station, Embsay, near Skipton, North Yorkshire BD23 6AX. Telephone: 01756 794727; talking timetable 01756 795189.
Glasgow Museum of Transport, Kelvin Hall, 1 Bunhouse Road, Glasgow G3 8PZ. Telephone: 0141-221 9600.
Gloucestershire Warwickshire Railway, The Railway Station, Toddington, Gloucestershire GL54 5DT. Telephone: 01242 621405.
Great Central Railway, Great Central Station, Loughborough, Leicestershire LE11 1RW. Telephone: 01509 230726.
Great Western Railway Museum, Faringdon Road, Swindon, Wiltshire SN1 5BJ. Telephone: 01793 466555.

Isle of Wight Steam Railway, The Railway Station, Havenstreet, Isle of Wight PO33 4DS. Telephone: 01983 882204; talking timetable 01983 884343.

Keighley & Worth Valley Railway, Haworth Station, Haworth, Keighley, West Yorkshire BD22 8NJ. Telephone: 01535 645214 or 647777.

Kent & East Sussex Railway, Tenterden Town Station, Station Road, Tenterden, Kent TN30 6HE. Telephone: 01580 765155.

Lakeside & Haverthwaite Railway, Haverthwaite Station, Ulverston, Cumbria LA12 8AL. Telephone: 01539 531594.

The Lavender Line, Isfield Station, Isfield, Uckfield, East Sussex TN22 5XB. Telephone: 01825 750515.

Llangollen Railway, The Station, Abbey Road, Llangollen, Denbighshire LL20 8SN. Telephone: 01978 860979; talking timetable 01978 860951.

Mid-Hants Railway – Watercress Line, The Railway Station, Alresford, Hampshire SO24 9JG. Telephone: 01962 733810.

Midland Railway Centre, Butterley Station, Ripley, Derbyshire DE5 3QZ. Telephone: 01773 747674.

National Railway Museum, Leeman Road, York YO2 4XJ. Telephone: 01904 621261.

Nene Valley Railway, Wansford Station, Stibbington, Peterborough, Cambridgeshire PE8 6LR. Telephone: 01780 784444.

Northampton & Lamport Railway, Pitsford & Brampton Station, Pitsford Road, Chapel Brampton, Northamptonshire NN6 8BA. Telephone: 01604 820327.

North Norfolk Railway, Sheringham Station, Sheringham, Norfolk NR26 8RA. Telephone: 01263 822045; talking timetable 01263 825449.

North Staffordshire Railway, Cheddleton Station, Cheddleton, Leek, Staffordshire. Telephone: 01538 360522.

North Woolwich Old Station Museum, Pier Road, North Woolwich, London E16 2JJ. Telephone: 0171-474 7244.

North Yorkshire Moors Railway, Pickering Station, Pickering, North Yorkshire YO18 7AJ. Telephone: 01751 472508; talking timetable 01751 473535.

Paignton & Dartmouth Railway, Queen's Park Station, Torbay Road, Paignton, Devon TQ4 6AF. Telephone: 01803 555872.

Peak Rail, Matlock Station, Matlock, Derbyshire DE4 3NA. Telephone: 01629 580381.

Pontypool & Blaenafon Railway, Big Pit, Furness Siding, Blaenafon. Telephone: 01495 792263.

Science Museum, Exhibition Road, South Kensington, London SW7 2DD. Telephone: 0171-938 8000.

Severn Valley Railway, The Railway Station, Bewdley, Worcestershire DY12 1BG. Telephone: 01299 403816; talking timetable 01299 401001.

South Devon Railway, The Station, Buckfastleigh, Devon TQ11 0DZ. Telephone: 01364 642338.

Strathspey Railway, Aviemore Speyside Station, Dalfaber Road, Aviemore, Inverness-shire PH22 1PY. Telephone: 01479 810725.

Swanage Railway, Station House, Swanage, Dorset BH19 1HB. Telephone: 01929 425800.

Swansea Vale Railway, Six Pit Junction, Nantyfin Road, Swansea Enterprise Park, Swansea. Telephone: 01792 653615 or 791001.

Swindon & Cricklade Railway, Railway Station, Tadpole Lane, Blunsdon, Swindon, Wiltshire SN2 4DZ. Telephone: 01793 771615.

Tiverton Museum, St Andrew Street, Tiverton, Devon EX16 6PH. Telephone: 01884 256295.

Welsh Industrial and Maritime Museum, Bute Street, Cardiff CF1 6AN. Telephone: 01222 481919.

West Somerset Railway, The Railway Station, Minehead, Somerset TA24 5BG. Telephone: 01643 704996; talking timetable 01643 707650.

Index

Locomotive engineers

Adams, W. 41, 45
Aspinall, J. A. F. 49, 70
Beattie, W. 41
Billinton, L. B. 26, 28
Bowen-Cooke, C. J. 10, 70
Bulleid, O. V. 13, 20, 22, 67, 69
Churchward, G. J. 10, 12, 25, 32, 52, 53, 54, 55, 72
Collett, C. B. 1, 11, 12, 32, 35, 48, 49, 52, 53, 55, 69, 72
Dean, W. 54, 69
Deeley, R. M. 8
Drummond, D. 8, 10, 45
Fairburn, C. E. 59
Fowler, Sir Henry 9, 15, 28, 43, 55, 68, 72
Gresley, Sir Nigel 14, 16, 17, 18, 25, 26, 27, 28, 32, 33, 34, 48, 51, 55, 66, 73
Hawksworth, F. W. 14, 16, 17
Hill, A. J. 48, 51, 67
Holden, J. 41, 48
Holden, S. D. 12
Holmes, M. 44, 64
Hoy, H. A. 53
Hughes, G. 70
Ivatt, H. A. 3, 41
Ivatt, H. G. 30, 32, 55, 56
Johnson, S. W. 8, 9, 41, 43, 63
Jones, D. 10
Kirtley, W. 5, 55
Marsh, D. Earle 50, 64
Maunsell, R. E. L. 9, 10, 12, 13, 27, 28, 29, 30, 34, 53, 56, 58
McIntosh, J. F. 10, 64
Park, J. 41
Peppercorn, A. H. 21, 22, 33, 40
Ramsbottom, J. 43
Raven, Sir Vincent 17, 34, 35, 60, 64, 70
Riddles, R. A. 22, 23, 31, 32, 39, 40, 55, 56, 57, 60, 61, 75, 76
Robinson, J. G. 10, 54, 61, 70, 72
Stanier, Sir William 14, 16, 17, 19, 35, 36, 55, 58, 75
Stephenson, Robert 5
Stirling, P. 25
Stroudley, W. 41
Thompson, E. 22, 33, 34, 35, 38, 40, 54, 58, 73, 74
Urie, R. W. 12, 34, 35, 45, 53
Wainwright, H. 9, 45
Webb, F. W. 64, 70
Whale, G. 70
Whitelegg, R. H. 68
Worsdell, T. W. 62, 64
Worsdell, W. 48

Locomotives
Western Region
Manor 4-6-0, 37
Grange 4-6-0, 37
Hall 4-6-0, 1
County 4-6-0, 17
Castle 4-6-0, 11
King 4-6-0, 11
4300 2-6-0, 25
4700 2-8-0, 32
1400 0-4-2T, 49
5700 0-6-0PT, 44
4500 2-6-2T, 54
6100 2-6-2T, 55
6600 0-6-2T, 50
4200 2-8-0T, 52
7200 2-8-2T, 52
2800 2-8-0, 72

Southern Region
Drummond T9 4-4-0, 8
Maunsell D1 4-4-0, 9
Maunsell Schools 4-4-0, 10
Maunsell King Arthur 4-6-0, 12
Maunsell Lord Nelson 4-6-0, 13
Bulleid West Country 4-6-2, 21
Bulleid Merchant Navy 4-6-2, 20
Billinton K 2-6-0, 26
Maunsell N 2-6-0, 27
Maunsell U 2-6-0, 29
Maunsell U1 2-6-0, 29
Maunsell S15 4-6-0, 34
Beattie 2-4-0T, 41
Adams 4-4-2T, 47
Adams O2 0-4-4T, 46
Drummond M7 0-4-4T, 46
Wainwright H 0-4-4T, 47
Stroudley A1x 0-6-0T, 42
Marsh E4 0-6-2T, 50
Wainwright C 0-6-0, 65

Billinton C2x 0-6-0, 65
Maunsell Q 0-6-0, 68
Bulleid Q1 0-6-0, 69
Maunsell W 2-6-4T, 57
Maunsell Z 0-8-0T, 53

London Midland Region
Midland Class 2 4-4-0, 9
Compound Class 4 4-4-0, 8
Patriot Class 6 4-6-0, 15
Jubilee Class 6 4-6-0, 16
Royal Scot Class 7 4-6-0, 15
Princess Royal Class 8 4-6-2, 19
Duchess Class 8 4-6-2, 20
Fowler 'Crab' 2-6-0, 28
Ivatt Class 4 2-6-0, 30
Black 5 4-6-0, 36
LYR 2-4-2T, 49
Ivatt 2-6-2T, 56
Fowler 2-6-4T, 58
Fairburn 2-6-4T, 59
Stanier three-cylinder 2-6-4T, 59
Ramsbottom 0-6-0T, 43
Park NLR 0-6-0T, 42
Fowler Class 3 0-6-0T, 43
Midland Class 2 0-6-0, 63
Midland Class 3 0-6-0, 63
Midland Class 4 0-6-0, 67
LNWR G2a 0-8-0, 70
S&DR Class 7 2-8-0, 74
Stanier Class 8 2-8-0, 75
Beyer-Garratt 2-6-0, 0-6-2, 67

Eastern Region
Peppercorn A1 4-6-2, 21
Peppercorn A2 4-6-2, 22
Gresley A3 4-6-2, 18
Gresley A4 4-6-2, 19

Robinson A5 4-6-2T, 61
Thompson B1 4-6-0, 38
Holden B12 4-6-0, 35
Raven B16 4-6-0, 34
Gresley B17 4-6-0, 14
Ivatt C1 4-4-2, 3
Ivatt C12 4-4-2T, 48
Wordsell J15 0-6-0, 62
Holmes J36 0-6-0, 64
Gresley J39 0-6-0, 66
Holmes J83 0-6-0T, 44
Thompson K1 2-6-0, 33
Gresley K2 2-6-0, 26
Gresley K3 2-6-0, 27
Thompson L1 2-6-4T, 60
Gresley N2 0-6-2T, 51
Hill N7 0-6-2T, 51
Gresley O2/2 2-8-0, 73
Thompson O4/8 2-8-0, 74
Thompson Q1 0-8-0T, 54
Raven Q6 0-8-0, 71
Raven Q7 0-8-0, 71
Gresley V2 2-6-2, 33

Ministry of Supply 2-8-0, 76

British Railways' Standard Locomotives
Britannia 70000 4-6-2, 23
Clan 72000 4-6-2, 23
Class 5 73000 4-6-0, 39
Class 4 75000 4-6-0, 39
Class 4 76000 2-6-0, 31
Class 2 78000 2-6-0, 31
Class 4 80000 2-6-4T, 61
Class 3 82000 2-6-2T, 57
Class 2 84000 2-6-2T, 56
Class 9 92000 2-10-0, 76